The Disappearance of Jamie Fraley

Pete Powers

Published by Trellis Publishing, 2021.

While every precaution has been taken in the preparation of this book, the publisher assumes no responsibility for errors or omissions, or for damages resulting from the use of the information contained herein.

THE DISAPPEARANCE OF JAMIE FRALEY

First edition. July 7, 2021.

Copyright © 2021 Pete Powers.

ISBN: 979-8224295210

Written by Pete Powers.

THE DISAPPEARANCE OF JAMIE FRALEY

PETE POWERS

Missing From Our Lives

When a person goes missing, the first twelve to twenty-four hours are the most crucial time. If the person is to be found alive, then it is during that first day when the best chance of a happy outcome exists.

More data exists on the make-up of missing people than of ways to trace them. Forty per cent of those in the US are children, and a third of the total are African American citizens. That is a heavy over representation. Only one in under eight people in the US are from this ethnic group.

Jamie Fraley is neither a member of the African American community nor a child, although at the time she went missing, the diminutive 22-year-old blond could have passed for one. Sadly, when she disappeared, she also did not turn up on the first day – nor the first year. In fact, 2018 marks a decade since the young woman was lost.

On Tuesday April 8th 2008 Jamie was not at her best. A touch of stomach flu had invaded her system, and she was suffering badly from sickness and pain. In fact, it was so uncomfortable that on the previous day she had felt ill enough to visit the hospital, not just once but twice.

Details surrounding Jamie's disappearance are sketchy; they were back in 2008 and today the authorities are little closer to solving the mystery than they were a decade ago. The bare facts with which they had to work are as follows:

Jamie was in her Gastonia, North Carolina apartment. This was in the 1800 block in Lowell Bethesda Road, a semi-rural lane with scrawny trees and mismatched houses. If not actually in her home, then police believe she was nearby.

Although the hospital had not admitted her, it is known that Jamie telephoned her mother at midnight, and told her that she was still feeling ill. Then, at 1.30 in the morning, Jamie called a friend and told her that she was really poorly, and that somebody was going to pick her up and take her back to the hospital. To police, the most useful element from this call to her friend was that she had to cut it short because she saw that 'he' had arrived.

Nobody heard from Jamie again.

Whether she actually set off for the hospital is unknown, but the evidence suggests that she did not. Her wallet, her purse, her keys and identification were found in the apartment. Maybe she was too ill to take them with her, and simply wanted to get to the hospital as quickly as she could, but that is unlikely. Another possibility is that she left her home expecting to go the hospital, but whoever took her returned her property to confuse police. Such a move cannot be ruled out, but would be a risky manoeuvre. The abductor could have been spotted, by a person or on CCTV. All that is certain in this bare case is that, whether she set off for the hospital or not, she never made it there. There are no records at all that visited the hospital for the third time.

However, one item of Jamie's was found outside her apartment, and that was her cell phone. A couple of days after she went missing, a worker carrying out maintenance on utilities discovered the device. It was a short distance from her home, on the intersection between East Hudson Boulevard and South New Hope Road.

Police carried out tests on the device, and discovered that several calls had been made from the phone at 4.30am on April 8th. But further investigations suggested that these calls were not significant in the search for Jamie. They had been made from Jamie's 'recently' called directory. Perhaps an animal could have been inadvertently responsible? Or could Jamie have desperately tried any way to contact friends and family to sound a warning about what was happening to her? Could the kidnapper even have taken the phone, been unable to use it and discarded it three hours after taking the young woman? Might Jamie have left her apartment, sick and uncomfortable, to wait for the person who was taking her to hospital? Perhaps she had been mistaken when she saw her lift arrive, and cut short her phone call to her friend. Had she then been attacked while she waited in the early hours of that moderately quiet street? If so, why had she not taken her keys, her wallet and her identification? Could the mysterious good Samaritan be a stranger to the area, and Jamie was waiting to show him (or her?) precisely where she lived? There were plenty of questions, but no answers. Even guesses were no more than stabs in the dark.

The absolutely final clue that police had to work with was a call made to the phone early the same morning, just four hours after her disappearance. That also led nowhere. By the time the phone came to the attention of the police, it had been too widely handled to be of any use in terms of a search for fingerprints.

And that was that. A meagre set of facts on which to work. An ill girl, definitely alive at 1.30am, maybe also at 4.30.

With so little to work on, police fell back on routine procedure. Most crimes against a person are committed by somebody who knows them. But even here, the police came up against a solid brick wall. The first suspect would be, under normal circumstances, the partner of the victim. As soon as they could be eliminated from the police enquires then they could start to look further afield.

Jamie Fraley did have a partner. But he had the best alibi possible to mitigate against him having carried out the abduction; on April 8th 2008 that fiancé was behind bars, locked away as a result of some petty crimes.

Cutting forward to 2015, it appeared for a short while as though there might be a breakthrough in the mystery. Despite annual appeals to the media, the case seemed certain to join those in the dank corridors full of boxes with 'Unsolved' stencilled on their lids. Then, a man already in prison for murder claimed responsibility for Jamie's disappearance. He stated that he had murdered the young girl, back in 2008.

Police were initially hopeful of putting the case to bed, even with such a dispiriting outcome. But they soon had their doubts about the validity of the confession. Jerry Douglas Case was serving 22 years for killing another person. Then, in 2012, he sent some correspondence to the Gaston Gazette in which he claimed to have killed a seventeen-year-old boy back in 1985. He had not been suspected in that case, but police investigated the man's claims and decided that there was enough behind them to re-open their investigation.

He was convicted of second degree murder for this crime. Not satisfied with that confession, Case contacted the newspaper once more, claiming responsibility for two more deaths. One was a Gaston woman who was shot dead in 2008, and the other was Jamie Fraley.

Whether Case was a fantasist, whether he wanted his name in the history books as Gaston County's biggest serial killer or whether he just enjoyed the distraction of police interviews and trials from his day to day life as an incarcerated nobody we do not know. Police showed interest in the confession for a short time. But the dates did not add up. Case was already in prison at the time of Jamie's death. It was not possible that she could be another of his victims.

Clues in this disappearance remain few and far between. In 2010 the tiniest of possible leads emerged. It really was very small, and very remote. Some teens were taking an illicit swim in one of the disused quarries that litter the Gateway Trail in the King's Mountain part of Cleveland County.

Chemetall Foote Corp quarry is a deep pool, a favourite place of youngsters risking an unsupervised dip on a hot and steamy day. But this group of boys discovered something that they had not expected. Some human bones lay stripped bare near the quarry, and one of the teens snapped the remains with his phone and showed the picture to his mom who reported it to police.

The bones were identified as human, and from what could be judged they did not show evidence of any traumas such as a breakage or gunshot wound.

At the time, there were at least four missing people in the Gaston County region. Asha Degree was just nine when she had disappeared from her Fallston home ten years previously. Mouy Tan had been seen near a school in 2008, she was 43. In the same year, Jennifer Rivkin's car was found abandoned in Gastonia, but the woman was never traced. She was another 43-year-old. The fourth person was Jamie Fraley.

The bones could belong to somebody who died accidentally, but the main trail in the wilderness park is popular, while the surrounding land is perfect for anybody seeking to hide a body. Butch Bridges was the ground keeper of the Gateway Trail in 2010.

'The rocky ridges and overgrowth make it a perfect place to hide a body, if that is indeed what happened,' he said. But, just like the outcome with every other lead, seemingly, in the Jamie Frayal case, this was another trail that soon went cold.

Jamie was a tiny lady. Just four feet eight or nine inches tall, and weighing in at just 95 lb, she was pretty, with blond hair and an innocent, girlish face. She was only twenty-two years old when she went missing, at a time when her life seemed to be getting onto an even track.

As a child, she had suffered from various bouts of mental illness, including anxiety and bipolar disorder. However, of late she had started to respond well to prescription medicines, and had begun to attend Garston College, although on a part time basis.

She was a caring young woman, her mother describing her as somebody who would always listen to the problems of others, always be ready to help. As is so often the case with such kindly but inexperienced people, she still, however, had some lessons to learn about life. In particular, explained her mother, that she could not always sort out everybody's problems.

When she met Ricky Simonds Jr, her life took on another turn forwards. They were very much in love, and planned to marry. She had his name tattooed on her ankle. However, as we saw earlier, Ricky and the police were common acquaintances. He was not a violent man, his crimes were not excessive, but he had a track record of petty offences.

Finally, when he was caught stealing, enough was enough and he was sentenced to a short spell behind bars – fifteen months in a state prison on a charge of theft. But Jamie stuck with her man, determined that she would remain loyal to him and convinced that under her influence he would soon get back on the straight and narrow.

She had also reached a point where she was able to start thinking about her future career. Her family said that her helping, caring side would be developed through the job she sought to take on, after her college was complete. She planned to work in substance abuse, counselling and supporting those who became addicted. It seems as though Jamie also had a strong interest in real life crimes and, ironically, missing persons. She was a keen user of the Myspace website, often posting under the name Jamie Simonds. Among the subjects she wrote about were JonBenet Ramsey and Samantha Rae Mendez. JonBenet was a six-year-old child beauty pageant queen who was murdered in the basement of her home while Samantha was a missing person from Gaston.

After her aborted visit to the hospital, the fact that she was missing was picked up quickly, but not within that crucial twenty-four-hour window. She had a meeting planned for the next day, and failed to turn up for it. Given that she was a reliable girl, not given to going out, or away, with telling people, her parents were worried. However, their fear revolved at this stage around the fact that she had been suffering from stomach flu. Certainly, the two visits to the hospital had resulted in her being discharged, sent home with some medication (collected by a neighbour – Jamie was a non-driver). But in her midnight call to her mother Jamie had expressed a fear that from whatever it was that she was suffering, it was not just the flu. Perhaps she had been right, and was in fact at home extremely ill?

Her parents visited her apartment, and were initially put at ease. Those personal items mentioned earlier – her purse, wallet; her keys and identification card lay where she kept them; there was no sign of a struggle and to all intents and purposes, Jamie had left her apartment willingly, wherever it was that she had headed to.

But panic started to grow as they tried to contact her. Nobody knew where to find her. Soon, the Frayal's decided that enough was enough. They contacted the police, and reported their daughter missing.

It is to the credit of the Gaston County police that they took the report seriously. The department committed three officers to the case full time, and all other members of its investigation team gave some thought and attention to identifying the possible whereabouts of the missing twenty-two-year-old. The contacted the State's Bureau of Investigation, and even went as far as to get in touch with the FBI. The chief detective on the case, Christie Rhoney said later: 'I have never seen a missing person case worked this thoroughly.' When Jamie's phone was discovered just over a mile from her apartment, a light appeared at the end of the tunnel. But as we know, that discovery led to nowhere, and that particular flame was soon extinguished.

Yet for all the dead ends, the trails that ended with nothing, police did have one lead. Not enough evidence for it to be regarded as anything more than being worthy of consideration, but it was the best that they had.

Ricky Simmonds, Jamie's boyfriend, was out of the frame. But his father was a different matter. He worked at the complex, looking after maintenance matters. That gave him greater access around the apartments than would be the case for others. More than this, he was one of the last people to have seen the young woman alive, when he drove her to the hospital earlier in the day before she disappeared, for her second trip there. He could not wait, and a neighbour brought her back.

Police suspected that he was most probably the good Samaritan who offered to drive Jamie back once more during the early hours of the morning. He lived just over the way from Jamie's apartment, in fact, next door but one. And as the father of her fiancé, he had gotten to know her well. Ricky Dell Simmonds Sr also had an unusual relationship with his son.

'We was friends more than we were father and son,' said the young man later. As a routine part of the police investigation, Simonds had been asked if he would sit a lie detector test, but he refused to do so. It would be wrong to draw too many conclusions from this; many people object to such invasions of their privacy. But if his reaction to this request was not that unusual, the father also had a dark history. The forty-nine-year-old had, like his son, spent time in prison. However, his crimes were somewhat more serious than those of his offspring. He had a record that included larceny, drug charges and fraud. He had also served time for manslaughter, having been inculcated in the murder of an ex-girlfriend, who had been discovered strangled. That was way back in the 1980s, but in June of 2008 a series of events conspired to suggest that Simonds Sr might not have completely changed his spots.

Another ex-girlfriend had filed for a restraining order to be placed against him because she believed he had broken into her car and stolen her purse and key. Kim Sprenger drove the car all weekend, without managing to pin down the dreadful smell that was getting worse by the hour. She assumed it was a dead bird caught somewhere in the engine, the corrupted fumes blown in through the car's ventilation system. Then, later, she had opened the trunk of her car, and made a surprising and extremely gruesome discovery. Because there, hidden in the trunk, was Ricky Dale Simmonds Sr, and he was quite dead. Police believe that he had broken into the rear compartment of the car, with the intention later of ambushing her...who knows why or for what? On his person were found the lost keys and purse, and it seemed as though having shut himself in the trunk of the vehicle, he had misjudged quite how incredibly hot it could become. He was unable to get out, and died from heat stroke. An unpleasant, frightening and painful death. Up until that time, Simonds had not been considered in any way a suspect in the disappearance of Jamie – he was her father in law to be if all were to go to plan, it would be like being abducted, probably murdered, by a member of your own family. There was no hard evidence linking Simonds to the crime. However, when it was reviewed circumstantial possibilities – evidence is too strong a term - existed to suggest that he could have been behind the kidnapping. Details remained sketchy, but were enough for police to list him as a person of interest in their enquiries.

Certainly, Jamie's mother Kim feels to this day that Simonds had some role to play in her daughter's disappearance. She fears that now she may never know the true whereabouts of her daughter, whether alive or, more probably, dead.

'I knew any questions we had for him, any information we could've got out of him, was gone,' she said, explaining that she had cried when she heard news of the man's death. Not tears of sympathy, or sadness, but tears of despair. 'He was hiding something, and we couldn't never get that out of him.'

Kim was not the only person to feel that Simonds Sr knew more about Jamie's disappearance than they ever knew. His son, too, believes that there is too much coincidence for there not to be a connection.

'First my fiancé goes missing,' he said, 'then my dad climbs in a trunk and dies? Does that make sense to anybody?'

If the police have found no success, and not for want of trying, in discovering anything about the whereabouts, demise or otherwise of Jamie Fraley, then plenty of others have done their bit to try to locate her. They still do.

One of the most significant of these is the support and investigative network, Missing Persons of America. Jerrie Dean is the Founder of both this group, and Missing Texas Forty. Formerly, she was a part of Federal Law Enforcement, but is now retired.

Her organisation had some positive news in 2015. A 'tip' was received, along with some photographs showing a woman alive and well. Jerrie thought that the photos could be of Jamie, and tried to contact both the local police and Jamie's family. However, both efforts proved to be in vain. Jerrie did not stop trying, and eventually made contact with Kim Fraley through a friend. She sent the photos, and Kim thought that they could well be of her daughter. However, the police did not agree.

They tried to check out the pictures in any case, but a long time had passed between the tip coming in and contact being made. If the pictures were of Jamie, she had moved on and the lead was lost. But, the development offers some kind of hope that he young woman might still be out there.

The case still remains open, and a reward of $5000 is on offer to anyone who can offer information that leads to the mystery being resolved, either with positive news or not. For Gaston County Police, the matter is still very much one they would like to solve, although they recognise that such an outcome is becoming increasingly unlikely.

In addition to Missing Persons of America, Jamie also features on other sites, such as Cue, which stands for Community United Effort. Stories from time to time surface in publications; they may jar a memory, or even reach Jamie, if she is still alive, and tell her that she is desperately loved and desperately missed. A Facebook page devoted to finding her has over seven hundred members.

Prior to the tip coming in to Missing Persons of America, Jamie's plight was given wider coverage when she was featured as a part of the Discovery Channel's 'Disappeared' series. In this, documentary films took a look at many cases where people had disappeared under strange circumstances.

On the basis that any good publicity is good publicity, such exposure was welcome news for Jamie's family, although once more, nothing of any use emerged from the film. In fact, this was the typical outcome for subjects featured on 'Disappeared'. During the series, over eighty cases of missing persons were examined.

As of 2014, fifty-seven of those people remained missing. Another seventeen people were discovered, but they were already deceased. However, for the eight people who were discovered alive, there was good news for their families and for them, at least in most cases. A couple of the missing whose whereabouts came to light were on the run from the police. Those two are now in prison, serving time for their various felonies. Another, Samantha Bonnell, was hit by and killed after she ran onto the road. The reason for her actions, which occurred in 2009, are unknown.

However, for five people – six per cent of the total number of missing persons featured – the news was good. Whether they would have been found in any case is hard to say, but for their families and loved ones, at least, there is the comfort of the knowledge that their relatives are safe and well.

Another, and perhaps the happiest story of all, is of Amber Gerwick, who disappeared from her loving family and four children as a result of suffering from a sudden, inexplicable bout of amnesia.

It seems certain that for Kim Fraley, Ricky Simonds Jr and other members of Jamie's family and friends, they will still be hoping against hope that something similar will prove to be the case for their missing loved one. As much as the odds are stacked against the best outcome happening, there is still a chance. But it remains extremely small.

Despite all of that. It is the task, the duty, the honour of a parent to never give up hope regarding their children. For Kim Fraley, that responsibility continues. Although, in her head she knows that, after being gone for a decade, the chances of finding her daughter alive are remote, and grow more distant with every passing month.

But that does not stop her believing that a chance exists for her daughter.

'Until somebody shows me different,' she says, 'I'm not going to think otherwise.'

So, Kim continues to work hard to uncover any clue regarding her missing daughter. Perhaps, she hopes, Jamie took off of her own free will, driven by some unknown need for time away from her loved ones. Perhaps Simonds Sr helped her to do that, this being the secret he would never pass on. Who knows? But now, with her daughter in her thirties, Kim hopes and prays that Jamie will decide it is time to return to her mother, or if that is impossible, at least contact her to let her know that she is well.

Occasionally, very rarely, stories emerge of people held against their will for years on end. Perhaps that is the fate of Jamie. Kim knows that any conclusion is pure speculation until hard evidence emerges. Even though logic says that her daughter is most probably dead, most likely killed within a short time of her disappearance, she continues to hope.

Her fiancé feels the same. 'I'm going to still hand out flyers,' he says with determination in his voice. 'I'm going to still look for her. I'm gonna do whatever I got to do. I love her. I'll always love her.'

That is the lot for family when a loved one goes missing. Only death or discovery eases the pain.

SUZIE AND STACY

KAREN BLACKSTONE

In June of 1992, two teenage girls who have just graduated from high school, Suzie Streeter and Stacy McCall went to Suzie's house to spend the night after a really long day of celebration and parties. They were looking forward to moving to the next stage of their life. Suzie's mother, Sherrill Levitt was at the house as well. All three of them mysteriously vanished in the middle of the night and they have never been seen again.

Decades later, the investigators are still working on this case, trying to put the pieces back together in order to discover what happened to them. It is one of the longest missing persons case in Missouri and even though the police received thousands of tips from the public, they are still unable to lock in on a single suspect or find any traces of the Springfield Three. This disappearance was extensively covered by the media in the years that followed. Each and every documentary that was aired did generate even more leads but it remains a cold case even to this day.

The background

Sherrill Levitt was a cosmetologist who worked at a local beauty salon and absolutely loved her job. She was born on November 1st, 1944 which makes her forty-seven years old at the time of her disappearance. Sherrill was divorced and had two children – one boy and one girl. She moved into the house on 1717 E. Delmar Street with her daughter Suzanne Elizabeth "Suzie" Streeter in 1992 but planned to renovate the residence and sell it for a higher price in a couple of months. The location was quite attractive and Sherrill knew that she would make some extra money if she put in the work. She would usually stay in after finishing her day job and spend her time refurbishing and improving various parts of the home. Sherrill was very close to her daughter but had a troubled relationship with her son Bartt Streeter. Sherrill didn't date anyone at the time of her disappearance but she did have a couple of ex-boyfriends who did not take the breakups really well.

Suzie was a bright and bubbly teenager who was excited to graduate from high school and follow her mother's steps in becoming a cosmetologist. She was born on March 9th in 1973 and was only nineteen years old at the time of the disappearance. Suzie used to live with her brother but decided to move back to her mother's place after a heated argument she had with him regarding his alcoholism. Stacy Kathleen McCall was Suzie's friend and they attended the same high school. Stacy had big plans ahead of her because she wanted to go to college once she graduates. She was born on April 23rd in 1974 and was almost one year younger than Suzie. The two used to be inseparable and would hang out with each other every single day when they were younger but they slowly drifted apart. However, they became close once again just a couple of months before the graduation.

The night of the disappearance

Suzie and Stacy graduated on June 6th, 1992 and Sherrill attended the ceremony. Later that evening, Suzie and Stacy were out, attending smaller graduation parties in Springfield, and hanging out with their classmates. They were joined by a third friend, Janelle Kirby and planned to have a sleepover at Janelle's house because they wanted to visit the water park in Branson, Missouri next morning. It was the perfect way to celebrate the end of high school and three girls were stoked to spend an entire day with their closest friends before going their separate ways.

However, the sleepover was canceled because when the girls arrived at the Kirby residence, they realized that the house is very crowded. Janelle's relatives were staying over and the girls didn't want to impose. Luckily, they had a good alternative. Suzie and Stacy made a decision to go to Suzie's house and then meet up with Janelle and her boyfriend on the following morning in order to go to the waterpark together. Each girl had her own car so they packed their belongings and drove to the house on 1717 E. Delmar Street sometime around 02:00 a.m. on June 7th. This was the last time anyone saw them. Since the change of plans was unexpected, Stacy didn't call her mother in order to inform her that they were going to Suzie's place.

In the meantime, Sherrill arrived home from the graduation ceremony and decided to spend her evening working on a dresser. She was trying to redecorate the house in order to get a higher price from the prospective buyers in the future. Sherrill talked to a friend over the phone until 11:15 p.m. and that was the last known contact anyone had with her before the disappearance.

We know that the girls did arrive at the Sherrill's house because their cars were parked in the driveway. The graduation gowns and clothes they had on that day were later found in Suzie's room and it appeared that they have taken off their make-up. Two used towels were located in the bathroom afterward which suggested that the girls washed their faces before going to bed. The beds were unmade so it looks like the girls did sleep there at some point but the investigators couldn't confirm it because teenagers sometimes leave their beds unmade and it wasn't a solid proof.

The aftermath

The girls were supposed to show up at Janelle Kirby's house sometime around 08:00 a.m. Janelle and her boyfriend Mike waited patiently but when they didn't show up, the couple thought that Suzie and Stacy overslept and they drove straight to Suzie's house in order to wake them up. When they arrived, they noticed the cars in the driveway which meant that the girls were still in the house. The couple didn't see anything out of the ordinary as they walked towards the front door. However, they saw a broken porch light and the glass was scattered all over the floor. The lightbulb was intact and it was on so they though that it was some kind of an accident. Mike swept up the glass pieces from the porch, threw them in a garbage bin as a favor, and didn't think twice about it.

The couple entered the house through the unlocked front door. They found Suzie's and Sherrill's dog, Cinnamon. The dog appeared to be slightly distressed. The home looked completely normal but they couldn't find anyone inside. There were no signs of struggle and furniture was in its place. They did notice the girls' purses, cigarettes, and other items inside but the house was empty, except for the dog. They stayed for a couple of minutes hoping that the girls went out to get some food. Janelle and Mike saw that the answering machine was blinking and that there were a couple of new messages on it. As Janelle and Mike were about to leave, the phone rang and Janelle answered it thinking that her friends were calling in. She heard a man's voice from the other side and he was speaking obscenities. Janelle hung up but the phone rang once again. She brushed it off as a prank call and the couple left the house. They thought that the girls definitely went to the water park without them so they decided to visit a local pool instead.

Stacy's mom, Janice McCall wasn't informed that the girls were at Suzie's house so she called the Kirby residence to talk to her daughter and make sure everything was alright. The Kirby's told her that the girls didn't spend the night there and that they went to Suzie's house instead. Sherrill did move into a new house recently so Stacy's mom had no idea where to call. Janice didn't have their new address or phone number. She managed to find the address through mutual friends and drove straight to the house. She arrived at the same scene as Janelle and Mike, saw the cars parked in front, and immediately had the feeling that something was off. Janice entered the home and searched around. She saw that there was a message on the answering machine so she played it right away. She also heard a man's voice who was saying very unpleasant things. The chances were that it was the same caller who spoke to Janelle earlier that day. Janice accidentally deleted the message which might have been a very important lead in this case. The origins of these anonymous calls were never discovered and the police were unable to trace them. Stacy's mom also points out that the television was on when she was at the house while Janelle was uncertain about this detail which means that someone might have entered the house in the meantime.

The friends and family gathered in the house during the afternoon and they made an assumption that the women left the house together in order to celebrate the graduation. But suspicion was growing and everyone was starting to get worried. The police were called in the late afternoon because Suzie, Stacy, and Sherrill were clearly missing and no one could locate them. The girls didn't go to the water park in Branson with any of their classmates and Sherrill was a no-show at her workplace. It is still unclear how many people entered the house before the investigators arrived at the scene so it was probably very contaminated.

The police talked to the people who were present at the scene and eventually left a note on the door for Sherrill asking her to call them back when she returns home. The call never came and the investigators returned to 1717 E. Delmar Street in order to take a closer look. The evidence inside the residence was quickly ruled out as unusable. They did discover a couple of clues that told them that the women probably left the house in the middle of the night under unknown circumstances. All three women's purses were found grouped together in Suzie's room alongside the car keys to three vehicles which were parked in front of the house.

The placement of these items was very odd. Police Chief Terry Knowles said: "A pack of Marlboros was on the night stand next to Streeter's bed; she was said to be a chain smoker. The television set was on. We have been told that Streeter was an insomniac, and it was only normal for her to have turned the TV on, and the sound down, to sleep." As previously stated, Sherrill was an avid smoker and she wouldn't leave the house without them. This piece of information was confirmed by Sherrill's son when he was questioned about the disappearance.

After one week of the investigation, police Chief Knowles addressed the public and said: "This case has gone beyond a missing-persons case. I think there has been some form of abduction." They knew they had to start looking for the suspects.

The list of suspects

The law enforcement faced a huge problem at the very beginning of the investigation because neither of the missing women had any ties to crime, drugs, or anything considered illegal. They were loved by everyone in their community and had no enemies. Kidnapping one person is incredibly hard but when three of them disappear at the same time, it is clear that something serious was going on. The police had to find the primary target but that was quite difficult.

The questions started to pile up because if Sherrill was the primary target, taking her from her home while there are two teenagers inside would be extremely risky. On the other hand, the girls weren't supposed to be at the house at all so if an unknown suspect targeted them, they had to follow their movement throughout the entire night after the graduation party.

The local media started covering this story and the photos of the missing women appeared on the TV the next evening. The police got plenty of phone calls and leads but the most interesting one came from a woman who lived close to Sherrill. She told the investigators that she was out on the porch on the morning of the disappearance and saw Suzie driving a very old van. The girl was clearly upset and the tears were pouring down her face. The van used her driveway in order to turn around and she heard a voice from the back telling the girl: "Don't do anything stupid." The eye witness didn't know any of the missing women but she recognized the crying girl as soon as she saw Suzie's photo on the evening news.

The police took this information seriously because it gave them a rough time frame when the women disappeared. It was obvious that someone got them out of the house sometime between 02:00 a.m. and

06:00 a.m. They even managed to find the same van and parked it in front of the main police station in Springfield, encouraging everyone to call if they had any information about the vehicle.

The detectives were confused because there were no signs of a struggle inside the house and it was obvious that a robbery wasn't a motive this time. The purses were intact and Sherrill's $800 were still in her wallet. The police started digging deeper into the case and focused on the relationships all three girls had in the past as well as the family members.

They immediately talked to Bartt Streeter who was Sherrill's son and Suzie's brother. He had a serious drinking problem at the time of the disappearance and it was known that his relationship with Sherrill and Suzie was rocky. He was a violent drunk and Bartt got into a fight with his sister a couple of months prior. Suzie returned to her mother and the two women cut all ties with Bartt. However, they couldn't find anything that would confirm that Bartt had anything to do with this case and he was quickly ruled out as a suspect.

They soon moved on to Dustin Recla who was Suzie's ex-boyfriend. The couple dated until March of 1992. He was arrested in February of 1992 with his friends Michael Clay and Joseph Riedel. They broke into Maple Park Cemetery in Springfield, entered the mausoleum and stole skulls and bones. The owner of a pawn shop called the police after three of them brought in the stolen gold fillings and the guys were charged with felony institutional vandalism.

It seems like Suzie was with them the night they robbed the mausoleum and was completely unaware of their intentions. She broke up with Dustin and provided the police with a statement that pretty much solidified the case against these three young men. There is no evidence that they were at the Sherrill's house and the only thing that is suspicious is Dustin's statement to one reporter in which he commented: "I hope they are dead."

The detectives couldn't find anyone suspicious who was directly involved with the missing women so they broadened their search. As the years went on, they weren't getting any closer to solving this crime. When Steven Eugene Garrison got arrested in 1993, a standard questioning took a whole new turn when Garrison decided to include some details related to the Springfield Three. He told the investigators that a friend of his confessed that he murdered the three women. Garrison did include a couple of details that were not known to the public at that time but the police couldn't find a solid connection to the disappearance. They did manage to identify Garrison's mystery friend and searched his property but didn't find any physical evidence related to this case. Steven Eugene Garrison is currently serving his 40 years sentence for raping and sodomizing a female student in 1993. If he confessed to being involved with the disappearance of the Springfield Three, he would likely face life in prison.

Robert Craig Cox

Robert Craig Cox was on the police's radar one week after the mysterious disappearance of the Springfield Three. Springfield was Cox's hometown and he moved back only a couple of months before. When the detectives brought him in for the questioning, he immediately announced that he had an alibi. Cox claimed that he spent an evening with his girlfriend and went to the local church early in the morning. His girlfriend confirmed the story but the investigators were still unconvinced.

Their suspicion was confirmed after Cox broke up with this woman. She told the police that the alibi was false and that Cox wasn't with her that night. His whereabouts were unknown at that point. Cox's parents entered the picture shortly after. They claimed that he slept at their place, providing him with the second alibi.

Robert Cox was arrested in 1997 while he was in Texas. He was convicted of kidnapping and a robbery. He began speaking with the authorities after his imprisonment, often referring to the disappearance of the Springfield Three. His statements were mostly vague and he refused to provide them with any solid leads. However, he did mention that "the three women were murdered and buried somewhere outside of Springfield." Cox continued to toy with the police, claiming that he would tell them everything about the Springfield Three and what happened on that night after the death of his mother.

Cox's modus operandi does match the possible crime that happened in Missouri. He is known for kidnapping his victims and holding them at gunpoint which was exactly what Sherrill's neighbor described. Cox is still a suspect in a murder that happened in Florida in 1978. He killed a 19-year old girl while she was going home from work. Cox was arrested after several years and brought to trial as soon as possible. However, the entire case against Cox went in a wrong direction and he managed to escape the death penalty. As a matter of fact, the Florida Supreme Court released him because they didn't have enough evidence to prove he committed the murder. Cox was released in 1989 but was transferred to California in order to serve a prison sentence over there. He was accused and found guilty of kidnapping that occurred in 1985.

Robert Cox is without a doubt one of the main suspects in the disappearance of the Springfield Three. He knew the city, was in the area at the time, and even though he has an alibi for that night, it is not a solid one. The investigators are still unable to directly link him with Suzie, Stacy, or Sherrill but it is known that Cox worked with Stacy's father at a local car dealership. He could have seen the girl there because she would often stop by in order to bring lunch to her dad. We might never know if Cox is teasing the police with his claims or if he is really guilty of this crime.

Possible burial sites

Cox Hospital in Springfield

Over the course of several years, police received thousands of tips from the public. They did investigate the majority of them but one tip related to their possible burial site stood out. South parking garage of the Cox Hospital in Springfield was still under construction back in 1992 and a couple of anonymous callers told the law enforcement that Suzie, Stacy, and Sherrill are buried underneath the concrete.

A break came almost ten years later when Kathee Baird, an investigating reporter decided to take matters into her own hands and contacted Rick Norland who is known for his work with the ground-penetrating radar. As a matter of fact, Norland worked with the US Government after the 9/11 in order to locate the victims who were buried beneath the rubble and the concrete so he had plenty of experience. He knows how to differentiate a body from sloppy construction work.

This device was used in solving dozens of high-profile cases as well because it allows you to search for any discrepancies or anomalies underneath the surface of the ground. Ground-penetrating radar cannot identify bodies with certainty but it can give you precise measurements of the anomalies in the structure underneath. An expert can tell if the radar discovered a grave or something else.

Rick Norland went to the Cox Hospital with Kathee Baird and they focused on a specific corner of the parking lot which was mentioned in the phone calls. Kathee Baird didn't disclose the details of the case and Norland had no idea what he was searching for or the number of the possible victims. The ground-penetrating radar immediately discovered three anomalies that roughly match the height of the missing women. The structure looked like a grave so Norland was fairly certain that three bodies are buried only three feet below the top layer of concrete. Two anomalies are parallel to each other, while the third one is positioned differently.

Baird and Norland went straight to the authorities with their discovery but the police were quite reserved, not trusting the information discovered by the ground-penetrating radar. They stated that they simply cannot break down the concrete with this lead only and that ground-penetrating radar might not be the most reliable way to locate the bodies. Cox Hospital was reluctant at first but they did give the permission to dig up the concrete if needed. The investigators made a decision to ignore this discovery and nothing has been uncovered so far. The police said that the parking lot was completed one year after the disappearance of the Springfield three so anything could have been buried in that spot.

Webster County

In the autumn of 1992, all major TV stations aired their specials about the Springfield Three. The public interest was growing and the police were once again swarmed with tips and calls from all over the area. One interesting lead prompted them to search a specific area located in Webster County which is fairly close to Springfield. The initial attempt to uncover any evidence from this lot was apparently unsuccessful. The police issued a statement claiming that they did find something but they cannot provide any more details at that time because they are still in the initial phase of the investigation. The law enforcement moved on to explore other tips and this lot was quickly forgotten.

Ten years later, Webster County became interesting to the investigators once again. The police received a tip but this time, two women claimed that at the time of the disappearance of the Springfield Three, the land was occupied by two men who were employed as construction workers. They also drove an old van that fit the description of the vehicle which was seen in the early morning hours by an eye-witness. The women who called in mentioned that men moved away two weeks after the disappearance.

Springfield police visited the property once again but they were unable to find any physical evidence of the missing women. The names of these two were never released to the public but we are sure that they are known to the people in charge of the investigation. It is still unclear if they are related to this case in any way but the coincidences are evident.

Both of them had the knowledge and possibly the access to the active building site at the Cox Hospital in Springfield. But they also had a large piece of land around their home where they could bury the bodies without being seen. A vehicle that fits the description of the van they drove in 1992 was seen with an upset girl behind the wheel. So many pieces fit perfectly but we still don't know if they are connected to the disappearance in any way or not.

So much time has passed since the disappearance of the Springfield Three that we might never get the real answers. Springfield Police is still working on the case but various crimes happen every single day. There are a couple of promising leads such as the parking lot at Cox Hospital in Springfield and the Webster County lot, but they need to be explored thoroughly.

THE COLD CASE OF LEAH ROBERTS

28

CHELSEA CROSS

When a loved one goes missing, the people closest to them who find themselves left behind often become consumed with the task of finding them. It is a relief to discover them, alive or dead, because then the mystery is solved, at least in part. However, when a person disappears and has yet to be found, what remains in place of them are the unanswered questions, worries, and strong emotions such as rage, guilt, sorrow, or unfathomable loneliness. The case of Leah Robert's is but one example of a missing person's case turned cold, with no new leads despite national attention and multiple re-dramatizations on shows like Unsolved Mysteries and Investigation Discovery. Her older sister and brother, Kara and Heath Roberts, are still searching for her although nearly seventeen years have gone by since her disappearance. Hopefully, someday soon, they will find answers.

Leah's white 1993 Jeep Cherokee had been found on March 18th, 2000. Some sources state that the vehicle was an SUV, which is a common contradiction in this case. Depending on which source you read can even affect how you feel about Leah as a person. With many unanswered questions, people have a natural tendency to fill in the blanks themselves. There were many clues in and around the Leah's vehicle, where her personal affects had been scattered about and left behind, but there was no sign of Leah. There are just as many unknowns as there are hints about what happened to her and where she could be. Among all the other mysterious circumstances surrounding her disappearance, there are hints of Jack Kerouac's influence. Kerouac, who was a Beat Generation novelist, is best known for *On the Road*, although Leah was also a big fan of another work of his known as *The Dharma Bums*. The latter novel depicts scenes of the area where her jeep was found and the former novel described a life of freedom from constraints, which begs the question: how closely might Leah have been trying to follow Kerouac's lead? Or was her presence in the area the product of something more sinister?

Her brother and sister might spend the rest of their lives looking for closure in their sister's disappearance. There is still a reward of $10,000 being offered for further information. Her siblings and the organization they have partnered with, Community United Effort, believe that even the coldest cases can be solved. It is important to remember that the answers might be difficult to hear: was Leah Roberts a victim of a kidnapping or murder? Was she mentally ill and simply lost herself in the expanses of a Washington forest or had she intentionally committed suicide? The evidence in her jeep, at least, tells us that she was not killed in the wreckage of her car, and so perhaps she managed to escaped a total of two car crashes during her life. However, by the time that her jeep had rolled several times over down a steep hill and into the forest, Leah Roberts may have already been dead. It is impossible to know for sure without someone coming forward with more details.

Early Life

Leah Toby Roberts had blue eyes and sandy blonde hair. She did not have an easy life. Although her childhood seemed normal for that part of Durham, North Carolina: a loving family with two siblings, Heath and Kara, for her to squabble and play together. Her grade school life also seemed average, and she obtained good enough grades to get accepted into North Carolina State University, which is when the first of the many tragedies in their lives struck: her family learned that her father had a serious, chronic lung illness. She was seventeen at the time, and despite the dark news, she was able to maintain her grades and stay in school that year. When she was twenty and working at completing her sophomore year at university, the second family tragedy struck: heart disease claimed her mother's life unexpectedly. In order to grieve and adjust to life after her mother, Leah took some time off of school. Shortly after returning to school in 1998, Leah was in a horrific car accident, in which her lung was punctured and her femur was shattered. She had an identifying surgical scar on her hip where a metal rod had been inserted in order to help the bone growth of her femur. When she awoke in the hospital, she claimed that she had gained a new lease on life. In order to recover, she again left school for a short time.

After these three bleak events shook up her life, Leah managed to press on with a new verve. She continued her education in Spanish and Anthropology, and was set to go to Costa

Rica for a field program in order to obtain higher fluency in Spanish. It was at that time that the final tragedy in her early twenties occurred. Her father died mere weeks before she was set to leave the country. However, she doggedly continued to prepare and leave for her trip, while leaving her mourning siblings behind to care for the estate. After the field program concluded, Leah spent a little longer in school before deciding that she would discontinue her program just before beginning her final semester. Both of her siblings urged her to stay in school for the final six months, but she could not be persuaded. Heath told reporters that he thought "that all of those things together had the cumulative effect of making Leah even more introspective and probably more aware that, although she didn't know what she wanted to do, I think she was unhappy that she wasn't achieving it." Her sister Kara, on the *Larry King Live* show, said to the audience and viewers that by "the time Leah was 22 she had lost both of her parents and here she is on the verge of graduating from college and I think she just felt lost and didn't have a lot of direction, and I feel like this took this trip as a soul-searching trip." A friend of hers named Susie Smith reported that "Leah is just a very awesome person. Everybody that meets her likes her. Very personable, great smile. But, you know, she was kind of private also. Definitely." These three comments paint a picture of an intelligent, insightful, and kindhearted young woman who was experiencing deep agony. Instead of staying in school, Leah seemed to completely turn her life direction around. She decided to pick up photography and guitar, adopting a kitten, and writing poetry in local coffeehouses. Somewhere in this time, Leah began to discuss her fondness for the novelist Jack Kerouac.

Road Trip and Disappearance

Shortly after she began to frequent the local coffee shop with her poetry, she made new friends such as Jeannine Quiller and her roommate, Nicole Bennett. Leah often discussed taking a trip like the ones detailed in Kerouac's novels with the other young women. Jeannine has said that "from the last conversation that we had, we were talking about *Dharma Bums* and about how Kerouac was up on Desolation Peak, just taking in all the beauty around him." This was the dream trip that her sister Kara now suspects was Leah's attempt to soul-search as she tried to recover from the five year span of shocking events and sudden losses. During her stints at the coffee shop, she wrote a lot of poetry, and she spent much of her time there reflecting on the meaning of life. Finally, in March, Leah and Kara had spoken to each other on the phone about what they were hopeful about in the coming year. Throughout this conversation,

Kara felt that things looked like they were coming around for Leah. Kara recollects that the two sisters had committed to seeing each other in the coming week when the phone call ended. Around the same time as that phone call, on March 9th, Leah and Nicole applied for a babysitting gig they would need to be at the following day. After that, Nicole left for work, and by the time she returned home, Leah's jeep was gone. Without school or a job, Leah's schedule had been sporadic, so Nicole did not become suspicious until Leah missed the babysitting shift the next day. Leah went unheard from on March 11th, again on March 12th, until finally, she was reported missing to the Durham police on March 13th by Kara.

Kara and Nicole went through Leah's belongings on March 14th in order to find some hints about where she might be. They found a note left by Leah that said: "I'm not suicidal. I'm the opposite. Remember Jack Kerouac." To end the note, Leah had drawn a Cheshire Cat's grin, which hadn't garnered any sort of significance in the press, even now. The other unusual part of the note is that Leah had left it in her room in plain sight, but not on the kitchen counter or on the fridge. For some reason, Leah had assumed that someone would be going into her room or through her possessions. This is also where she left her portion of the rent for the upcoming month. Among the missing was Leah's kitten, although no one knew for sure whether or not Leah had taken her along until later. During her trip to Costa Rica, Leah had given Kara the power of attorney over her bank accounts, which Kara also used to try and determine what was going on with her sister. There were gas station entries as well as motel rooms and other small purchases and larger cash withdrawals, which traced a trail to the northwest. However, after the card was used to buy gas on the 13th,the usage of the card stopped. Despite no new purchases, at that time no one had any reason to suspect that Leah had met with foul play. Once Kara came into contact with Leah's friend Jeannine and spoken to her about their mutual love for Kerouac, Kara felt reassured that she knew Leah's plan and went back to her own day to day life. However, on March 18th, Kara expected a Happy Birthday phone call from Leah, but never received it. Instead, on that day, she received a letter from the Durham County sheriff's office in her door's mailbox with instructions to call the Whatcom County Sheriff's office in Bellingham, Washington. Upon making that call, Kara was suddenly faced with the fifth tragedy in her young life. After her father's diagnosis, her mother's death, Leah's car accident, her father's death, Kara now had to deal with Leah's disappearance and potential death or suicide.

The car was discovered by two joggers who came upon several articles of clothing tied in trees, although some sources allege that the clothing was merely hanging off of the tree branches. They then followed the scattered clothing along a trail down a treacherous embankment to a white jeep, which was in poor condition. It was off the side of a small road named Canyon Creek Road, which connected to the Mount Baker Highway, which leads to some residences and logging camps at the base and throughout the Mount Baker-Snoqualmie National Forest, which is located a small ways south of the US-Canadian border. Leah was not there when the jeep was discovered, the jogging couple had not seen any signs of her in the area besides the strangely placed articles of clothing. Kara and Heath flew out to meet investigators in Bellingham in order to aid with the search and further investigation.

The Investigation

The jeep had been traveling approximately 40 miles an hour when it left Canyon Creek Road and crashed into the forest. Investigators were able to determine the speed of the vehicle by examining the damage done to it and the nearby vegetation. The insides of the jeep had clothing and pillows set up and placed about as if the vehicle had been used as some sort of shelter, however, the other contents were thrown around and jumbled up, which are traits of a multiple rollover event. Kevin McFadden of the Whatcom County Sheriff's Office said that the driver should have been injured: "With the speed that the vehicle was traveling and the amount of damage to the vehicle, you would anticipate some type of injury to the person inside. At least some type of evidence to indicate contact damage, that the person had been inside the vehicle ... we brought in dogs, we brought in search and rescue, and did a complete grid search up and down the road. But they weren't able to find any indication that anybody had left that vehicle." For some reason, someone had placed the pillows and clothing to form a shelter, but did not pickup the scattered belongings of Leah, some of which included quite a bit of cash ($2,500) and jewelery. Her guitar and cds were also untouched. A small cat carrier and some food were also on the sign, which indicated that Leah had brought her kitten with her. Like Leah, Bea the kitten has never been found. An important clue was found in her belongings as well, which helped investigators understand when she arrived in the area, and that was an innocuous ticket stub

for the movie American Beauty on March 13th, which aired at the Bellis Fair shopping mall. That meant that Leah had purchased gas in Oregon and then spent a few hours in the town after the 5-6 hour drive. Besides the fact that her belongings were spread-out everywhere around the crash site, there were none of the signs of the blunt force trauma that normally come standard in a multiple rollover style car crash such as fractured glass or blood, however. Since then, there has been evidence found of the starter being tampered with, which lends itself to the suggestion that the vehicle was empty when the accident occurred.

After Kara and Heath arrived, they began to ask questions in the neighboring town of Bellingham and passed out papers with Leah's picture and information on them. They spoke to businesses where Leah might have gone, although the amount of cash found in her jeans pointed to her buying very little in the town. They headed to the only sit-down restaurant that the Bellis Fair Mall offered, because Kara had an instinct that Leah may have eaten there before or after seeing the movie. The restaurant management led the officers to two men, one of whom claimed that Leah had left the establishment with a man named Barry and created a sketching of him for the police. None of the other patrons or the other man could verify whether or not Leah had actually left with someone, but police did note that on the security footage obtained from that gas station in Oregon, Leah kept searching the parking lot as if someone had been waiting for her. Unfortunately, the gas station had not had security cameras monitoring their parking lot, although officers do believe that there was no one else in the car with her.

One of the biggest indicators to police that Leah had met with foul play was the engagement ring that they had found under the car mat in her car. The ring belonged to Leah's mother, and she never went without it, as it served a constant reminder of her mother. Her roommate Nicole Bennett also knows about the ring: "As long as I've known Leah, she has worn her mother's engagement ring. It was her most prized possession. And when we discovered that the ring had been found in the car, it was definitely, for me, a bad sign." Those close to Leah have gone on record as saying that she wouldn't have taken it off unless she felt she had to, or if she was completely unaware. Some have suggested that Leah may have been in a fugue state, which is officially known as Dissociative fugue and is classed as a DSM-5 Dissociative Disorder. Normally fugue shapes are temporary and last from a few hours to to days, but there are rare instances in which they can last for months. These fugue states are often accompanied with sudden travel and establishing a new identity. There is a lot of parallel between the DSM-5 definition and Leah's case, with a few small differences including the fact that Leah had planned the trip somewhat substantially. Although in Oregon she was considered to be in good shape, a man had called in a panicked sighting of Leah in Everett, Washington, which is likely when she was last seen.

What We Know Now

Since the day of the accident, the widespread area where Leah disappeared has been subject to repeat searches by cadaver dogs and metal detectors, looking for the metal rod that Leah had had put in when her femur had shattered. The *Unsolved Mystery* show aired a segment on her disappearance back in 2001, when its segment still played on Lifetime. None of the tips that came as a result of the broadcast led the investigators to anything worthwhile. Kara teamed up with Monica Caison, who is an expert in solving cold cases by drawing consistent media and national attention to them. On a now annual basis, Kara and Caison organize a caravan through Caison's organization, Community United Effort, which travels the route Leah had likely taken during her fateful trip. They both went onto the Larry King Live, and Kara told the viewers: "I don't really know how I would have made it through the past five years without [Caison] ... We're just trying to, you know, keep Leah's face out there as much as possible."

Near the time of the Investigation Discovery airing of Leah's case in 2011, two investigators had been handed the care of Leah's vehicle, which Kara had asked the police station to protect. They found new evidence that had been ignored in the original investigation. There was a male's DNA on Leah's clothing, and they were the investigators who noticed that the starter relay in the jeep had been altered. The alteration made it clear that Leah did not have to be in the car, nor no one had to be, in order for the vehicle to continue acceleration until its demise. The investigators noted that the man who had originally told investigator about the mysterious third man, named "Barry", had been a mechanic and ex-military. They began to suspect him, and they made actions to get his DNA and fingerprints examined, but he had moved to Canada in the years since the initial investigation, which made the process more difficult. By the time the *Disappearance* episode on Investigation Discovery had aired, the fingerprints had come back negative and the DNA had yet to be processed. He has allegedly commented on online forums protesting his innocence.

Kerouac's Influence on Modern Youth

Jack Kerouac's writing and lifestyle have had an obvious influence on Leah and her missing persons case. He is known as an author of the Beat Generation, and he is likely the most famous. Although his writings were largely anti-capitalistic, very quickly his novels became very popular, and the bohemian lifestyle depicted within morphed into a

Hollywood-style spectacle. Years later, however, these ideas of Kerouac returned to the youth they were originally meant for, and inspired Leah to take her road trip. Even during the height of Kerouac's popularity, his ideals were heavily criticized and served as scapegoats for many of the political problems of the age. It seemed as though the thoughts expressed within *On the Road* were offending everyone who wasn't a beatnik. That said, he influenced Bob Dylan's political flare as well as newer writers and philosophers like Sven Birkerts and Thomas Pynchon. Students all over the country were reading him in the 60s and 70s, despite *On the Road* not being added to the curriculum until much later. The novel addresses the dissatisfaction with mainstream culture that some factions of America possess, and has remained as part of the cultural background ever since. Multiple editions have been published since the original, each honoring some facet of the novel—the original manuscript, for example, or a marked anniversary.

Into the 21st century, the book remains a heavy influence of counter-cultures such as hipster, dust punk, and the bohemian lifestyle, which brings us back to Leah Roberts. On the Road, among Kerouac's other works, remains a steadfast influence on the youth of today who are unable to cope with the pressures of modern American society. Although Leah was seemingly a part of the mainstream that counter-cultures reject, the sudden loss and traumas that she had experienced in such a short time span might have parallels with the pressure to achieve. Leah was maintaining her grades throughout adverse circumstances, and there is no way of telling how much pressure she was applying to herself, but the sudden decision to drop out of university so close to it being finished acknowledges that she was under considerable stress. The freedom from stressors that life on the road offered must have been very tempting for her.

Conclusion

Mysteries and missing persons' cases are equal parts thrilling and chilling because they could happen to anyone. In 2012 alone there was upwards of 700,000 missing persons cases in the United States and at any one time there are approximately 90,000 persons missing on average. Of those 90,000, two thirds are adults, and there is a relatively even gender split. About half are white, which includes Hispanic ancestry. Unlike Leah Roberts' case, however, most missing persons in the United States are found. Although the first day or two are the most integral, and it may be that Leah's case had been reported too late. It is actually rare for someone to disappear without a trace, which makes Leah's case all the more unusual and frightening. Perhaps if she had kept a more regular schedule, her friends and family may have been more concerned about her road trip. Her face remains a national news icon, and her sister and brother are still actively searching for her, even if her file has gone cold. It is hard to answer why she hasn't been found yet, and there are still too many unsolved riddles regarding her disappearance.

Leah had many reasons to be depressed or mentally ill, but so did her sister and brother. It is likely that she did not commit suicide, but the possibility is still there. Why did she suddenly drop out of university? Up until then, she seemed to be a highly motivated individual, despite having to miss a few semesters of school due to personal tragedies. The investigators have gone on record saying that "you can't rule out foul play when you don't see somebody for over a year, but there's no evidence to indicate that that has happened. We did process the vehicle for your typical evidence, hairs and fibers and blood, but there was nothing to indicate that happened." Could Leah have been kidnapped or murdered a long ways away from her vehicle and the crash site? Many online commenters suggest that perhaps Leah made herself a new person and has kept out of the national spotlight, despite how difficult that would be in the modern age and considering that her attempt to disappear would have been most likely caused by a fugue state. Some have suggested that Leah wanted to live as free as Kerouac did within his novels, although her sister Kara doubts that theory: "I can understand Leah's needing to get away and find some peace within herself, but considering the loss that our family's experienced, it's difficult for me to think that she would leave us open for another loss like this." Likely, Leah wanted a Kerouac-inspired vacation from her society and instead she met with yet another horrible tragedy.

STALKED & ABDUCTED : THE TRUE STORY OF BRIANNA MAITLAND

KENDRA HICKS

There are approximately 2,300 United States citizens reported missing every single day. Some of these are runaways, some are misunderstandings, some are hurt or killed, and other just disappear without a trace. The friends and families they left behind are left with just a glimmer of hope that their loved one may one day turn up, which is oftentimes more painful than the closure of knowing your child or friend is in a better place.

Missing persons cases are a popular subject matter for shows like Criminal Minds or CSI: Crime Scene Investigation, but many real life cases don't end in the happily-ever-after seen on primetime. In the real world, these cases are often full of loose and dead ends, muddied by apathetic law enforcement or unclear communication between the victim and those close to them. Of those that go missing, the majority are women, who often present themselves as an easy target for those looking to inflict harm on another.

On March 19th, 2004, Brianna Maitland disappeared. The 17-year-old girl had just left the Black Lantern Inn in Montgomery, Vermont, where she washed dishes and occasionally served tables, when her car was found abandoned only twenty minutes later. Despite a brief visit from a local police officer, and curious passersby photographing the abandoned Oldsmobile, she was not reported missing for several days. Her parents, Bruce and Kelli Maitland, assumed she was at home, and Brianna's roommate was out of town at the time. Brianna left a trail of clues behind her, but over 12 years later there is still no official story for what happened that night. As the years pass without any major leads, the investigation has petered out and will soon be coming to a close.

Who Was Brianna Maitland?

Brianna Maitland was born and raised in Burlington, Vermont, where she spent the first seventeen years of her life living at her parents' quiet farmhouse. On her seventeenth birthday, she packed up her belongings and moved out on her own, despite her parent's pleas for her to stay another year. Her mother told interviewers that there was no serious issue or conflict that resulted in this decision, but that her daughter was fiercely independent and prematurely ready to venture into the world on her own. Although Brianna's early departure caused many to suspect an unhappy childhood or home life, she and her parents appeared to maintain a good, somewhat close relationship for the months after her move.

Brianna was an attractive girl, easily looking several years older than her young age. She was brunette and slightly petite, at 5 foot 4 inches and about one hundred and ten pounds. All around, she seemed to be a well-liked girl with many friends. Some rumors emerged after her disappearance regarding her moving to a new school district. These rumors blamed the move on Brianna being bullied relentlessly by other girls at her original high school, which motivated Brianna to pick up and move her life to an entirely different area. While these rumors are persistent, Brianna's parents or friends haven't confirmed them at this point.

At first, Brianna moved in with her boyfriend, James, wanting to be closer to a group of her friends that lived over 15 miles away from her parents' community. Moving in with her then-boyfriend seemed to be more a move of convenience than love; it didn't appear that she moved out of her parents' house with the intent of being closer and more codependent with him. She enrolled in a new high school, the same one as these friends, and began to settle into her new living situation. Unfortunately, her new home life was quickly uprooted by arguments with James, who she had accused in letters of having a severe drinking problem. By February 2004, barely a month before she would disappear without a trace, Brianna had dropped out of school and moved to a new house.

Now living with Jillian Stout, a friend she had known since early childhood, Brianna attempted to regain control of her life. The two young girls shared a modest home in Sheldon, Vermont, and seemed to be doing fairly well for themselves. Brianna enrolled herself in a high school equivalency program, hoping to earn her G.E.D. as soon as she would have earned her high school diploma if she had not dropped out. Brianna was reportedly excited about this test, looking forward to a new chapter of her newly independent life. Despite the hardships she had fallen on after moving from her parent's house, Brianna was determined to pull herself up and support herself on her own. Sadly, she would disappear only hours after finishing her exam.

While Brianna was not known as a serious troublemaker, she did drink and party like so many other teenagers do. At one of these parties, only three weeks before the night of her disappearance, Brianna was assaulted by another girl from her high school. At the hands of this girl, named Keallie Lacross, Brianna suffered a broken nose and concussion. Some rumors surrounding this attack suggest that Kaellie or one of her friends felt threatened by the pretty Brianna when she was seen talking to their boyfriend or a boy they were interested in. Although Brianna did press legal charges against Keallie, these were not yet resolved when she disappeared, so they were dropped several weeks later.

This scene cast light on some of the darker sides of Brianna's life. Her boyfriend was likely and alcoholic if not worse, she was bullied and harassed by other girls in her social circle who disliked her, and she likely partook in drugs and alcohol herself. While this isn't unusual for a 17-year-old, many in the community and police force expressed doubt that Brianna was attacked or hurt in some way. Instead, to them, she was just another burnt out, teenage runaway.

The Morning of Her Disappearance

The morning of Brianna's G.E.D. examination, she and her mother, Kellie Maitland, met for breakfast. Kellie reported that there was nothing out of the ordinary at this time, and that she had sent her daughter off to her test with plans to meet up and celebrate with her later.

For her celebration, Brianna chose to go shopping with her mother in the afternoon. Kellie said that shopping was one of her daughter's absolute favorite things to do. She said Brianna could walk into any store, pick the most "avant gard" piece off the rack, and model it like she was on an international runway. Brianna's sense of style was something her mother and many others admired about her. In television and print interviews, Kellie Maitland retells these memories with a clear fondness, holding onto those last final hours she spent with her daughter in 2004.

However, according to her mother, Brianna's shopping trip was cut short. As they were waiting in line to check out at one of her favorite stores, Kellie said that Brianna's attention was caught by something outside the store window. Saying that she would be right back, Brianna left the store. Kellie is unsure where he daughter actually went; she said that she never saw Brianna enter another storefront on the street. After paying for her items, Kellie exited the store and found Brianna waiting for her at their vehicle. She had no shopping bag from another store with her, and there was no one else nearby that Kellie thought she could have been speaking to.

There are many speculations as to what, or who, drew Brianna Maitland out of the store that morning. No matter what happened, Kellie said that her daughter was visibly upset the entire car-ride home. Wanting to respect her daughter's privacy, Kellie never asked Brianna what had happened earlier that afternoon, but this would be the last time she ever spoke to her beloved daughter. She dropped Brianna off in the driveway of her and Jillian's shared house, and then turned onto the highway to the quiet farmhouse she and Brianna had once both called home.

At home, Briana started getting ready for her Friday night shift at the Black Lantern Inn, one of the teenager's two minimum wage jobs. At around 3:30 in the afternoon, Brianna left her house in her 1985 Oldsmobile, leaving a note for Jillian assuring her that she would be back home after her shift was over. Jillian found the note when she arrived home, after Brianna had already left for the Inn, but then went away for the weekend without ever hearing from Brianna again.

The Last Known Sighting

The Black Lantern Inn, founded in 1803, closed its doors for good on March 29th, 2015. Remnants of the Inn's events and menus can still be found on Facebook and outdated travel sites. The most recent post on the Black Lantern Inn's Facebook page simply says, "The Black Lantern Inn is closed." The Inn offered an Irish restaurant and brewpub, which featured the Inn's own small batch beer brewed on location. Located in Montgomery, Vermont, a small town nestled between the East Coast's rolling mountains, the Black Lantern Inn drew a combination of loyal locals and transient tourists to its establishment. With a fireplace and public house feel, the restaurant and brewpub offered a cozy retreat for the perfect stag night or romantic getaway on a cold winter night. This is where Brianna Maitland spent her last documented hours.

Friday nights are notoriously busy in the restaurant and service industry, and March 19th, 2004, was no exception. In fact, it was even busier than expected, keeping the staff on their feet for the better part of the night and filling the back of house with dirty dishes and utensils. Backed up on her work, Brianna stayed several hours later than usual in order to finish washing the entirety of the night's dishes.

Sometime during the evening, Kellie and Bruce Maitland passed the Black Lantern Inn, hoping to stop in and visit Brianna at her new workplace. However, after seeing how busy the restaurant was, and not wanting to embarrass their daughter in front of her coworkers and boss, they continued on their way home. To this day, Kellie regrets not making that stop, if only to see her daughter one last time.

At 11:20 that night, the Inn's staff members were finally done with all of their closing duties. As per restaurant tradition, they all planned to hang out, have a drink, and relax after a hard night's work. Brianna, however, declined, stating that she needed to get to bed in time for her Saturday morning shift at her other job in nearby St. Albans, Vermont.

As far as Brianna's coworkers reported, she left alone from the Black Lantern Inn in her usual ride, her mother's hand-me-down Oldsmobile sedan. Brianna and Jillian's home was about twenty miles outside of Montgomery, but Brianna's vehicle didn't make it further than a mile from the Black Lantern Inn. And, as far as anyone knows, perhaps neither did Brianna.

Shortly after 11:30 that night, a man driving down Route 118 reported seeing a seemingly empty car parked at a run-down building, known as "the old Dutchburn house." He said the headlights were on, but he didn't notice anyone inside or near the exterior of the vehicle. A little after midnight, another report came in of a stopped car at the Dutchburn house, this time with a turn signal on. Later in the night, at about 4 a.m., an ex-boyfriend of Brianna Maitland noticed the vehicle parked off the road as well. Finally, early the next morning, a group of travelers stopped to examine the oddly abandoned vehicle, even going so far as to take photographs of the unusual scene.

A Delayed Investigation

Daylight revealed that the vehicle had actually been backed into the Dutchburn house, damaging the wooden exterior. By early afternoon on March 20th, a Vermont State Police officer finally arrived at the scene, deeming the car abandoned and having it towed to a local salvage lot. It wouldn't be until March 25th that the oddly abandoned car would be identified as Brianna's Oldsmobile.

Because of a series of unfortunate circumstances, no one noticed Brianna's absence until Tuesday, the 23rd, when Jillian called Kellie Maitland to ask if she had heard from Brianna. Since she was away all weekend, Jillian just assumed that Brianna had made other plans and had simply not returned home yet. It is unknown why her second job, which she was scheduled to work Saturday morning, did not question her absence. It's possible that they just thought she was another teenager pulling a no-call-no-show, too apathetic to formally quit.

As soon as Kellie heard that her daughter had been missing for several days, she began calling everyone she could think of. Despite trying to contact her friends, employers, and other family, Kellie failed to find any information on where Brianna could be. With no leads to go off of, she called the local police to file a missing persons report.

At this point, Brianna's Oldsmobile had been removed from the Dutchburn house almost five days ago. That Thursday, March 25th, Kellie and Bruce drove to the Vermont State Police in St. Albans to submit photos of Brianna with her report. It was then that an officer showed them the photos of the abandoned Oldsmobile on Route 118, and the Maitland's identified the vehicle as Brianna's.

As the news of Brianna's disappearance broke, questions began to emerge as to why the officer sent to investigate the Oldsmobile had not raised an earlier alarm. The Oldsmobile had been littered with all kinds of Brianna's personal belongs both within and outside of the vehicle, including: two uncashed paychecks, her purse, jewelry, spare change, a water bottle, and, perhaps strangest of all, a lime slice. Vomit, assumed to belong to Brianna, was also found in the car's front seat. News articles, personal bloggers, and other armchair detectives have accused the officer, seemingly unnamed in any public documents, of complete negligence when handling the Brianna Maitland case.

While the Vermont State Police conducted a several month long investigation, they held onto the belief that there was no foul play involved in Brianna's disappearance. The general consensus was that she had run away or been swept up in some kind of substance abuse. Brianna's friends and family continue to believe that she would not abandon her life and belongings like that.

In 2012, a young woman's skull was found on a Vermont highway, showing signs of age and being exposed to the elements for several years. While no conclusive evidence has been able to tie this discovery to Brianna or one of the other missing women in Vermont, it remains a possible sign of her fate.

Recently, on the twelfth anniversary of Brianna's disappearance, law enforcement revealed that they had collected DNA evidence from inside the abandoned Oldsmobile. It is unknown if this DNA solely belonged to Brianna, or if this was new evidence or had been collected during the initial investigation. There have been no public updates related to this potentially new evidence.

Brianna's family maintains a Facebook page dedicated to remembering her and encouraging others to come forward with information about her or other missing persons. Support for Brianna and her family continues to flow in through comments and pictures posted to the page.

Flurry of Theories

Unsolved mysteries, whether they be in the form of everyday murder or the paranormal, are a popular pastime for the average armchair detective. Brianna Maitland's case is no exception. There is no limit to the number of rumors and theories built up around her disappearance, some more believable than others. While there is no official statement on what actually happened to Brianna at this time, by breaking down the most prominent theories we can begin to understand what might have happened that night. While this list is not inclusive of every theory about Brianna's disappearance, it features the most likely or those that are most supported by the case's evidence.

A Drug Deal Gone Bad – One of the more common theories regarding Brianna's disappearance connects the scene of her abandoned car with the shopping incident reported by her mother. It is known that, like many girls her age, Brianna was often seen at parties where alcohol and other substances were being used. Whether Brianna had an issue with any particular drug is unknown, but it's very likely that she partook at least occasionally, and she regular hung out with teenagers who were known drug users and dealers. These facts lead many people, including some police officers, to believe that Brianna was caught up in a bad drug deal or otherwise got on the bad side of some of the area's dealers.

The most common story within this theory is that Brianna owed money to a local cocaine dealer, who she had been avoiding for some time. When out shopping with her mother earlier on the day of her disappearance, Brianna had spotted this dealer or one of their associates following her and her mother around town. This is when Brianna had gone outside, confronting the dealer and possibly promising to meet him later on with the money he was owed.

Later that night, either because the dealer was simply sick of waiting for his money or because Brianna attempted to avoid him once more, things turned violent. What happened after Brianna's car was abandoned is not entirely answered by this particular theory, but it is clear serious harm was done to Brianna Maitland that night or shortly after. Later, a story would emerge that filled out some of this theory's more gruesome details.

Murdered by Ramon Ryans – About three years after Brianna's disappearance, a police report from the Burlington Police Department offered to potentially solve the mystery. This report, given by Debbie Gorton, from Colchester, Vermont, claimed to answer the questions that the Maitland family and law enforcement had been asking for years.

Gorton's statement came about because her sister, Ellen Ducharme, had been charged with the drug-related murder of Ligia Collins. Some speculate that this story was an attempt to throw attention off of Gorton's son, who had recently been arrested for an unrelated crime, but that question remains unanswered.

In Gorton's statement, she claimed that Ducharme had told her about the murder and disposal of Brianna, committed by Ducharme and several of her associates. According to Ducharme, a known drug dealer, named Ramon Ryans, had taken a "couple thousand" dollars from Brianna which she had given him to buy crack cocaine. Brianna, either because she decided she needed the money for something else or because Ryans failed to deliver on the deal, confronted Ryans to ask for her money back. Ducharme told Gorton that Ryans had abducted Brianna on the night of March 19th, when her car was found abandoned.

Ducharme told Burlington police that Brianna was kept alive for up to a week, suffering who knows what kind of emotional and physical abuse at the hands of Ryans and his friends. Brianna was kept in Ryans basement, possibly even past the time of her death. According to Ducharme, Briann's body was dumped at an unknown local pig farm.

It is particularly strange, if this is truly what happened, why Brianna's attackers did not take her money or un-cashed paychecks from her vehicle. If her murder was motivated by money, these would be easy loot. More likely, though, this was a crime of pure rage.

Gorton believed that several people were involved in the murder and disposal of Brianna's body, including her sister, Ramon Ryans, Moses Robar, Darrel Robar, and Timothy Crews. No charges were ever made against these individuals in the case of Brianna's disappearance and the accusations remain uncorroborated by any local law enforcement.

Stalked at Work – It is sadly common for service industry staff, especially women, to be harassed and followed by their customers. While Brianna's primary role was in the back as a dishwasher, she occasionally served and helped out in the front of house when it was busy.

Another common theory of her disappearance is that she had acquired a stalker in her time at the restaurant, or from somewhere else who had then found her workplace and continued his stalking there. Since Brianna was an attractive, young girl, this theory is not too hard to believe.

Perhaps Brianna was aware of this stalker, though never confided in the police or her loved ones, and this is who she had seen outside the store she was shopping in with her mother. If she had confronted this man and demanded that he leave her alone, this would have made her nervous and on-edge like her mother later described. This rejection by his object of affection may have also sent the stalker into more violent methods.

With this theory, some believe that the man was hiding in her Oldsmobile's backseat, waiting for Brianna to clock out and head home. Shortly after she had left the Black Lantern Inn, he could have emerged and told her to either pull over or drive somewhere at his command. This also would have explained why the Oldsmobile was backed into the old Dutchburn house, because oftentimes women are instructed to drive into an object in order to stun or hurt an attacker in their vehicle. Unfortunately, if this is what happened, it appears that the stalker was successful in his pursuit of Brianna.

Pregnancy Scare – Fueled by the small town rumor mill, another frequently heard story is one of teenage pregnancy. Playing up Brianna's partying side, this theory suggests that a mistake between two young people turned into a case of cold-blooded murder.

On the day of her disappearance, Brianna already knew that she was pregnant. Maybe she had just found out, or maybe this fact had been weighing on her mind for weeks. Either way, when she left her mother in the store checkout line, Brianna was going out to tell someone about her pregnancy. Whether this was a friend or the potential child's father, Brianna did not want her mother to overhear the conversation and find out that she was pregnant.

Later that night, she had stopped at the old Dutchburn house. The vomit found in her vehicle leads some to believe that she got sick on her way home from work and pulled over in order to clean up or gather herself before continuing home. This is where someone met her, because she asked him or her to or because they had followed her from the Black Lantern Inn, most likely the potential child's father. Either way, this person was extremely unhappy at Brianna's news. Perhaps it was a cheating partner who had gotten Brianna pregnant, or simply a young man who was nowhere near ready for the financial and emotional responsibility of having a child.

The old Dutchburn house is backed by a nearby forest and river, which can be easily accessed by a short walk. If Brianna was killed at the location of her car, this is likely where her body was left. No trace of Brianna was ever found in this area, but there is always a chance that it was swept away or buried beneath the soil.

A Deadly Party – Following along with Brianna's supposed party girl image, this theory suggested that she had actually made it further than the old Dutchburn house that night. However, as we'll see, there are some discrepancies throughout this theory that make it highly unlikely.

After leaving for work that Friday, rather than going home to rest for her morning shift like she had told her coworkers, Brianna had driven out to a nearby party. Here she was either involuntarily drugged or willing took drugs herself. As the night progressed and intoxication levels increased, Brianna began to overdose. Unable or unwilling to get her the appropriate help in time, Brianna died that night at the party. Afraid of being caught, and potentially charged with the murder of Brianna, those at the party secretly disposed of the body. Later that night, her car was planted in order to look like it had been abandoned or that something had happened to her on the side of the road. If a couple drunk teenagers were driving Brianna's vehicle to the old Dutchburn house, this could also explain the vomit found in the passenger seat of her car.

The most obvious hole in this theory is the sightings of Brianna's parked car at the Dutchburn house less than an hour after she had clocked out of work at the Black Lantern Inn. This timeframe would leave her no time to get to a party, let alone overdose and have her vehicle planted by other partygoers. However, witness sightings are notoriously inaccurate, leading some to believe that the initial sighting of Brianna's Oldsmobile either didn't happen, was a different car pulled over on the side of the road entirely, or happened at a later hour and the witness was either mistaken or lied to the authorities.

For those who see Brianna as a wild, high school drop out who ended up hanging out with the wrong crowd, this story might be very easy to believe. Even law enforcement were quick to say that Brianna's disappearance was more likely an accident than premeditated foul play. Brianna's close friends and family don't believe this tale, though, and hold onto the belief that Brianna was an innocent victim the night of her disappearance.

A Victim of Human Trafficking – Human trafficking is an often overlooked issue in the United States, with many believing that it only occurs in foreign, third world countries in Asia or Europe. While most known cases of human trafficking occur at airports, large metropolitan areas, and other locations with a high volume of travellers and business, some do occur in small towns or seemingly innocuous places like coffee shops or malls.

Women are the most common victims of human trafficking, usually being sold into the non-consensual sex trade. While the men, or "Johns," who visit these women are rarely aware that the sex worker they are visiting is actually being held against their will, these women's captors can be violent, abusive, and frequently end up killings their prisoners. Some human traffickers will also force their victims to develop a drug addiction, often to heroin and other hard street drugs, so that they are more easily manipulated and apathetic to their situation.

Those who believe that Brianna, likely targeted because of her petite, non-threatening figure and good looks, was sold into sex trafficking believe that she was smuggled over the nearby Canadian border. This would explain why her personal belongings, such as I.D.

and jewelry, were left behind; the abductors would not want any identifiable information with her in case they were caught. However, it's strange that none of her money was taken if this was the case.

Final Blow From Kaellie Lacross – While Kaellie Lacross's, the girl who had attacked Brianna at a party just three weeks before her disappearance, charges were eventually dropped, she remained the primary suspect in many people's eyes. After all, it is quite possible that a grudge strong enough to assault someone over is a grudge strong enough to murder someone, purposely or not, over.

Whatever it is that triggered Kaellie's attack at the party, it's not impossible to believe that she wasn't satisfied with the outcome. If Kaellie was intending to teach Brianna a lesson, whether it was to not speak poorly or her or to stay away from particular boy, she might have felt the need to scare Brianna even further. Knowing that Brianna worked at the Black Lantern Inn, Kaellie could have followed her and forced her to pull over on the side of Route 118.

Here, Kaellie, likely the help of her peers, could have threatened Brianna and physically attacked her again. Whether this attack was meant to kill Brianna doesn't matter, only that it eventually did. Realizing that they had made a huge mistake, and would now be charged with not just assault but with murder as well, the group quickly disposed of her body. They could have placed the body in another vehicle, taking it to a different location, or carried her back into the secluded woods behind the old Dutchburn house.

If the motivation behind this attack was only to scare Brianna, then they would have had no interest in taking her money or other belongings. This theory is supported by having a clear motive, though there is no official report on what the conflict between Brianna and Kaellie was, and if it was serious enough that Kaellie would gone through the trouble of practically hunting Brianna down to resolve it.

The Mystery Remains

Despite this exhaustive list of theories, there is really no way of knowing what happened to Brianna until someone comes forward with new information. As the Maitland family and Montgomery community approach the thirteenth anniversary of Brianna's disappearance, there are plans to scale back the search for her and what happened.

Up until now, the Maitland family and Vermont State Police have funded a $20,000 reward fund for any information that leads to the discovery of Brianna Maitland, but after all these years with no solid leads, the plan is to donate the fund to a missing persons advocacy group sometime in 2017. Although the Maitland's have not given up hope, they are ready to take a step forward in grieving their daughter, no matter what has happened to her.

The Brianna Maitland Facebook page remains active, wishing followers happy holidays and posting alerts for other missing persons cases. Serving as a memory of Brianna, whether she remains alive or not, the page aims to draw out information on her case and the thousands of other missing persons cases that go unsolved every year. Brianna's case has also been featured on several true crime podcasts, television shows, and blogs, hoping to unearth the answers to questions that everyone has been asking since that cold night of March 19th, 2004.

THE DISAPPEARANCE OF KELSIE SCHELLING

ANA BENSON

Every time a woman goes missing or is found murdered, the police usually takes a closer look at their spouses or boyfriends. It is a standard procedure, especially if there were indications that they were in a troubled relationship. The disappearance of Kelsie Schelling is one of the biggest mysteries in Colorado. This young pregnant woman was last seen in February of 2013 and the case is still open to this day.

However, Kelsie's family was quite disappointed at the lack of interest by the police to investigate her then-boyfriend Donthe Lucas, who was clearly involved in this crime. After all, Donthe did invite Kelsie to his hometown on that fateful night and he was the last person who saw her alive. When they realized that the police are stalling with the investigation, the family made a promise that Kelsie's case will not be forgotten until they discover what really happened. They kept the public informed through their Facebook page and eventually managed to reach the Colorado Bureau of Investigation.

Early life

Kelsie Jean Schelling was born on 18th February 1991 in Holyoke, Colorado. She grew up in a tightknit family and later became even closer to her mother after the divorce of her parents. Kelsie was only eleven years old when they split up but she would often talk to her father as well. However, they didn't see each other that often because he moved to a different part of town. After graduating from high school, Kelsie attended Northeastern Junior College located in Sterling, Colorado. She was fascinated with psychology and planned to major in it once she gets accepted to the university.

Kelsie was friendly and outspoken, so it comes as no surprise that she had many friends and was a life of every party. During her time at Northeastern Junior College, Kelsie met Donthe Lucas. He was a star player on the basketball team and the two of them fell in love instantly. Donthe Lucas had a very difficult childhood and he grew up in Pueblo, Colorado which is an infamous place known for higher crime rates than anywhere else in the state. He loved basketball and it was clear that he would be an outstanding athlete even in high school. Basketball players do have enormous salaries so Donthe Lucas did see it as an opportunity to help his family out further down the line.

He was hoping that a scout would attend one of his games and recruit him for one of bigger colleges or universities that had a good basketball team. But his big break never happened. Instead, he ended up in Northeastern Junior College which was alright, but Donthe wasn't quite happy with that outcome. His dissatisfaction was evident even in the relationship with Kelsie. Their romance had constant ups and downs, and the two of them would break up, and get back together which drove Kelsie mad. They did finally call it quits after several semesters, and didn't see each other for quite some time.

After finishing the two years at the junior college, Kelsie pursued her education even further, and she moved to California to attend Vanguard University in Costa Mesa. She was finally able to study psychology full time. Donthe continued to play basketball for Emporia State University in Kansas. Kelsie's family was happy she managed to end her relationship with the troubled basketball player, and they hoped that she would make a new life far away from Colorado. Kelsie was independent and she enjoyed living and studying in California. When she wasn't attending classes, Kelsie worked at a tanning salon with her best friend. However, she did drop out of the college because the school work was a bit too much for her at the time and her only option was to go back home. She moved to Denver in 2012 and started working in a store. Meanwhile, Donthe Lucas was back in his hometown Pueblo.

The two of them started talking once again during the autumn of 2012. It was obvious that they still had feelings for each other, so no one was surprised when Donthe and Kelsie decided to spend the Christmas holidays together. The couple seemed happy to everyone around them, but Kelsie did tell her friends that their relationship was still very toxic. Donthe was still treating her badly, calling her names, and starting unnecessary fights. Soon enough everything will change. A few weeks after the holidays, Kelsie found out that she was pregnant. Shocked at first, Kelsie was lost and decided not to tell anyone for a couple of weeks. But keeping a secret was hard. So she called her mother and told her the news. Kelsie's mother Laura would later say that even though her daughter felt a bit stressed, she was still excited about the pregnancy. Yes, she was young but Kelsie was determined to make it work.

Donthe Lucas didn't take the news so well. Having in mind how dissatisfied he felt about his failed basketball career, it is not wrong to assume that the news about a baby simply solidified the fact that his dreams will never come true. Kelsie noticed the change in his mood and openly told him that he doesn't have to be a part of their baby's life. But it is also worth mentioning that Kelsie confided in her best friend that Donthe was ecstatic to become a father at one point. However, his mind was constantly changing. Kelsie went to see her doctor on 4th of February 2013 and he confirmed that she was eight weeks pregnant. The baby was healthy and doing well. The doctor provided her with an ultrasound of the unborn baby, and she was full of joy. Kelsie immediately sent out the pictures to her mother, her friends, and Donthe. Unfortunately, the excitement will not last forever.

The night of the disappearance

Donthe and Kelsey exchanged several emails on February 3rd, 2013. He invited her to visit him in Pueblo. She turned him down saying that she needs to go for a checkup the next day to make sure everything is alright with the baby. After seeing her doctor on the morning of February 4th, 2013, Kelsie went straight to the store. She worked the second shift and was expected to come home sometime after 10:00 PM that night. However, she was in contact with Donthe for the entire day, texting back and forth about the pregnancy. Donthe told her that she should drive out to Pueblo after work because he had a surprise for her. Not knowing what it is, Kelsie asked for more information because Pueblo is two hours away from Denver, and she would probably be tired after work. He insisted that she would be happy with his surprise and that he cannot tell her anything over the phone.

It is safe to assume that Kelsie thought that Donthe was ready to change and start a family with her. Their relationship wasn't a standard one but it seemed like Kelsie was willing to move past all the negative things and focus on the future. So after her shift ended, Kelsie got in her Chevy Cruze LTZ and drove to Pueblo in the middle of the night. Donthe was supposed to meet her in a parking lot in front of a local Walmart. The surveillance cameras did confirm that Kelsie got there on time, but Donthe was nowhere to be seen. She waited in a parked car for almost an hour before sending another text message to Donthe, saying that she has been in the parking lot for too long and that she would come pick him up at whatever location he is at the moment. She got a reply sometime around 12:15 AM.

Donthe told her that he will be waiting for her in the street next to his grandmother's home. Kelsie is seen exiting the parking lot a couple of minutes after she got the message. She clearly did arrive at the second rendezvous spot, but once again Donthe wasn't there. Kelsie sent him another message asking where is he and Donthe replied that he will be there in a minute. This is the last known communication between these two until sometime before 04:00 AM. After going through the phone records, police did discover that Donthe called Kelsie at 03:54 AM but she didn't pick up. The significance of this mysterious phone call will be revealed later. After reviewing the cell tower pings for both phones, the investigators did discover that they were in close proximity to each other.

The search for Kelsie

Kelsie's mother Laura got really worried the next day because she wasn't able to reach her daughter over the phone. She tried calling numerous times but it went straight to the voicemail. The last message she got from her daughter was the ultrasound image of her unborn child, and Laura wasn't sure if something happened to Kelsie after work, or she was ignoring her calls. Laura contacted Kelsie's friends who told her that she went to Pueblo to meet with Donthe. With no word from her daughter, she called Donthe who picked up his phone and told Laura that he had seen Kelsie last night, but that she drove back home in the morning.

Laura was starting to panic, but she did tell Donthe that she would involve the police if she doesn't hear from her daughter soon. Laura and Kelsie were very close and they did tell each other everything, but she suspected that her daughter kept this information from her because she didn't want Laura to know that she was meeting with Donthe. After all, Laura was aware of the nature of their relationship, and his reluctance to accept the baby. Plus, Laura would probably advise Kelsie not to go to Pueblo in the middle of the night.

Laura contacted the local law enforcement and told them that her daughter was missing. Without any solid leads or evidence, they started asking around for Kelsie. Their first step was to take a closer look at Donthe because he claimed that he was the last person to saw Kelsie. She did travel from Denver just to see him. After checking Kelsie's credit card records, they did notice that the card was used hours after Kelsie's last known contact with Donthe. They reviewed the surveillance of the ATM and noticed that Donthe had the card and picked up $400 from Kelsie's account. They weren't sure if Donthe had Kelsie's agreement to use the card, but that was a felony in the state of Colorado, so he was led to the police station for questioning. He had a lot of things to clear up, starting with the timeline of Kelsie's visit to Pueblo.

Donthe's interview

After being picked up by the police, Donthe told his own version of the story. They did see each other that night and talked until early morning hours. Donthe and Kelsie got into a fight and she felt too agitated to drive back home to Denver. She was also very tired from working the second shift. Instead, Kelsie decided to sleep in her car which was parked near his grandmother's house. According to Donthe, his phone rang sometime around 07:00 AM and it was Kelsie. She wasn't feeling well and asked Donthe to drive her to a hospital. He put on his clothes, got to her car, and drove her to the Parkview Hospital.

Kelsie wasn't sure if something happened to the baby during their argument last night and she insisted to see a doctor before she heads out to Denver. Donthe sat inside her car in the parking lot for two hours when she finally emerged from the hospital. Kelsie told him that she had lost the baby. She then asked Donthe to drive her to Walmart to get something to eat and buy some snacks for the road. The two of them started fighting while they were in Walmart and Kelsie refused to drive him home. Donthe simply walked away and got to his grandmother's house on foot. He didn't see Kelsie later in the day and he assumed she went home. He didn't mention stopping at the ATM to pick up the money during his initial interview.

The investigators did notice a couple of possible leads that could collaborate Donthe's story, namely the Parkview Hospital. Each medical facility keeps detailed records of the patients they treat. After speaking to the staff and going through the data, they have confirmed that Kelsie didn't check in during the morning of February 5th. There were also numerous surveillance cameras all over the building and none of them picked up Kelsie entering or leaving the hospital. It was obvious that this part of Donthe's story was not true.

Of course, the police investigators decided to check out Walmart as well because the parking lot and stores do have surveillance cameras, and they might have picked up something that would be of use. While they couldn't find Kelsie or Donthe entering the Walmart, they did notice Kelsie's car on the parking lot. However, the timeline didn't match up with Donthe's story because Kelsie's car appeared at noon, and not in the morning. Plus, Donthe was the only passenger in the car.

Another surveillance camera which was positioned on the back side of Walmart did record Donthe getting into his mother's car – another detail he failed to mention in the initial talk with the investigators.

Without any proof that Donthe's version of the events is true, they called him up for a second interview. The investigators did have a plan this time - they wanted to find out more about the ATM, and how it fits into his timeline. He told the detectives that he took $400 in order to pay his bills and that Kelsie lent him the money since he was at the ATM while Kelsie was at the hospital. When the detectives told Donthe that there is no record of Kelsie ever being in that hospital, his reply was: "I don't even know what to say right now."

They also presented him with Walmart surveillance video that proves Donthe was the only person in the car. He was surprised with the evidence put in front of him, and before the detectives managed to get him to open up, he decided to lawyer up. He was only charged with the identity theft due to the fact that he used Kelsie's credit card, but the case was dropped. The judge had determined that Donthe did use Kelsie's credit card in the past and it was a normal behavior. However, nobody managed to figure out why Donthe had her card in the first place. After all, if Kelsie decided to ran away and start a new life, she would need the money, as well as her vehicle.

Speaking of Kelsie's car, the investigators took a closer look at the surveillance video from Walmart parking lot because they wanted to follow the vehicle. Exactly one day after Donthe left Kelsie's car there, another man approached the car and got inside by using the key. He didn't break in or steal the car. The man was dressed in black, wearing a hoodie, so identifying him was almost impossible. His body type was different than Donthe's, and the mystery man was significantly shorter. Keep in mind that Donthe was a tall basketball player, so his height would be noticeable, even in a low-quality video.

Seeing the direction in which the car went, the police collected the surveillance videos from stores and businesses which were in close proximity. They put the puzzle pieces together and found a route but they couldn't follow it all the way. One day later, the car was dropped at the parking lot of Saint Mary Corwin Hospital. The man locked the car and walked away. The investigators located the vehicle on 14th of February, 2013 and figured out the timeline. But nobody knows where the car was during 6th of February. There weren't any signs of a struggle that would indicate that Kelsie was killed in her car. Almost all of her personal items were missing, including her wallet and a backpack.

While it is unclear if the vehicle was tested for the traces of DNA, an unnamed police officer who worked for Pueblo Police Department will later say that they did find bodily fluids in the trunk of Kelsie's car, as well as two palm prints. However, no one knows what happened with this evidence and was it ever tested. It is simply another thing which the police investigators decided to ignore in this case. Unfortunately, the whole investigation will be under scrutiny soon after.

Theories

Figuring out a solid theory without too many evidence or information can be challenging. Laura, Kelsie's mother, claims that her daughter was probably murdered and that it was premeditated. The first red flag for her was Donthe's initial invitation to meet him before the doctor's appointment. When Kelsie refused, he knew that he had to act fast. Donthe lured Kelsie to Pueblo by saying that he has something to show her, but he never gave an explanation to the law enforcement about what the surprise really was.

It is clear that Kelsie was alive and well up until the point she met Donthe in the street next to his grandmother's house. This is where the trail goes cold. The activity on her phone stops until 04:00 AM. If we analyze the location of the phones, another theory is that Donthe led Kelsie to a remote location and harmed her. It was possible that Kelsie dropped her phone in the middle of a struggle. Donthe couldn't find the phone in the dark, so he had to call her number. He was very likely getting rid of the evidence.

There is a possibility that the two of them did indeed get into a fight, and that an unfortunate accident happened. However, it is more likely that Donthe planned to get rid of Kelsie, and had planned every single step he would take that night. He really insisted to see her as soon as possible. While it is not fair to put the blame on the rest of Lucas family, the fact that his mother picked him up immediately after he left Kelsie's vehicle at the Walmart's parking lot indicates that she knew what was going on. Pueblo Police Department did stop investigating Donthe, and they claimed they didn't have enough physical evidence to prove that a crime really occurred. But they did receive a couple of noteworthy tips which were ignored and never pursued.

The missed opportunities

The entire investigation of the disappearance of Kelsie Schelling was troubling from the very beginning. While the detectives did not have physical evidence of a crime, it was clear that Donthe was the last person who saw Kelsie alive. In every standard investigation, he would have been the prime suspect, and the investigators would do their best to find more proof that he was somehow connected to the crime. The cell tower pings did show that both of their phones were in a remote area next to Pueblo in the early morning hours.

But there are even bigger missed opportunities that could have provided the investigators with the proof they needed. For instance, Donthe was living in his grandmother's house at the time of Kelsie's disappearance. However, the entire family moved out soon after. The landlord started redecorating the house because he wanted to rent it again. He did hear about the missing girl from Denver but had no idea about the details of the case, or the fact that the Lucas family was involved in any way.

He decided to put the new carpets in and when he lifted the old one, the landlord noticed a strange stain on the bottom. He contacted the police enforcement because he was worried that something bad has happened in the house. However, the police ignored his request to check out the stained carpet, and no one had ever arrived at Lucas' previous residence to pick it up. The landlord ended up throwing the carpet away because he simply couldn't keep it forever in the house and wanted to move on with the renovation.

Another missed opportunity involved a couple of fishermen who were out on a lake on a night fishing expedition. It is important to mention that the lake was located near the Saint Mary Corwin Hospital. As you might recall, that was the spot where the police officers discovered Kelsie's vehicle on the 14th of February 2013. They were out on a bank when a hook got stuck to something poking out of the sand. The fishermen went to investigate and were sure that they saw a part of a human ribcage, as well as a skull.

They were terrified by that discovery and left the area right away. Both of them were reluctant to notify the police because they did have some troubles with the law in the past. But that didn't stop them from telling this story to their friends who urged them to contact the local law enforcement. A couple of months passed before they finally talked to the police, but the lake wasn't searched afterward.

The current searches

Family and friends continued to search for Kelsie even after it was clear that the police enforcement forgot about her case. They created a Facebook group that was constantly updated with new information. Pueblo Police Department did go through many changes after Kelsie went missing. The lead investigator was replaced with a new one who was willing to cooperate with the Schelling family. The Schellings did offer a large reward for any new leads that might help them locate their missing daughter. The reward was $100,000 at one point.

This eventually led to false claims and misleading messages such as the one which claimed that Kelsie was still alive, but was placed into a sex traffic ring after a hired hitman decided not to kill her.

Laura Schelling contacted the police and told them about the message. Since the investigators decided to follow every lead possible, they dug deeper and even involved the FBI. Their experts did manage to trace the message back to Russia through the IP address so it was clear that this tip was useless.

The biggest break in the case happened in the spring of 2017 when Colorado Bureau of Investigation finally got the authorization from the local law enforcement to join the search. CBI did determine that the prime suspect should be Donthe Lucas, and they got the warrant to search the area around his previous place of residence. A large number of police officers was seen around that house during April of 2017, and they dug up the parts of the backyard using heavy machinery.

The search has been successful and the officers left the scene carrying bags of evidence. However, they stated that they didn't find any traces of Kelsie's remains. Kelsie's family released the following statement after the search: "The past 2 days have been grueling and emotional, ending with the outcome we did not hope for. Kelsie is still missing. There is no way for me to convey to you all the pain that I feel right now. Sincere, heartfelt thanks goes out to the members of Pueblo PD, CBI and Parks & Rec who worked so hard on this search for Kelsie. This was a physically demanding excavation for them and we witnessed how hard they worked. Despite all the issues we have had in the past, the new leadership over Kelsie's case from PPD and active involvement from CBI is giving us hope that an effective investigation is finally taking place."

The case is still active and the police didn't arrest Donthe. But the positive changes are happening and Kelsie's family is certain that they will find the answers they are looking for now that the investigation is finally moving forward.

THE DISAPPEARANCE OF BRITTANEE DREXEL

82

FAITH TORINO

Brittanee Drexel disappeared from Myrtle Beach, SC while on spring break on April 25, 2009. She was 17 at the time and traveled without receiving parental consent. She told her mother that she was staying at a friend's house near their home in Rochester, New York. Brittanee's mother, Dawn, then learned where she really was when her boyfriend, John, called her after he suspected something had happened to Brittanee. Her parents immediately grew angry, scared, and devastated when they received word that their daughter was missing.

Brittanee was born on October 7th, 1991 and lived in Rochester, New York. She moved frequently during her youth as her father was in the military. She was a junior at Gates-Chili High school and the year was a rough one with her parents separating. She would live with her mother but still see her father frequently.

She was blind in her right eye and had several surgeries to correct her hyperplastic primary vitreous. To keep her eye from wandering, she would get contacts that made both eyes look the same.

Britt was described by friends and family as a smiling, fun-loving girl. Her demeanor had changed by her junior year in high school as she was depressed that her parents were separating. She would sleep in late and begin to skip school. She would overdose two times on her mother's pain medication and both times were fueled by the fact that she had just broken up with her on-again, off-again boyfriend, John Grieco.

"I felt it was all my fault," Brittany's father said. "When I was here none of this went on. She didn't ingest as many pills as they thought but still watching her get her stomach pumped was a warning. I need help."

"I remember the look on her face," Dawn said. "She was all red. She was crying, tears coming down her face. 'Why would you do this? Nothing in life is that bad.'"

Brittanee would be forced to see a counselor after the suicide attempt. Still, things seemed as if they were a mess on the home front.

Her parents were separating and her mother was losing her home. But she would resume her studies at school and excel on the soccer field.

"She was fast," her father said. "Her coach would say he'd never seen a girl that fast."

By the time Spring Break rolled around in, she was ready to go on an adventure with some of the older kids she knew. It was a long-standing tradition for Rochester students to go to Myrtle Beach for vacation. Britt wanted to enjoy the night life and lay out in the beach, so when one of her older friends asked if she wanted to come along she didn't hesitate.

She asked her mother first and the idea was immediately shot dawn. Dawn Drexel did not know any of the friends that would be taking Brittanee.

"She asked me and I said 'no,'" Dawn recalled. "Then she went to talk to her father. She would play us both. She would say Mom said 'no' but Dad said 'yes.'"

Brittanee was determined to go. She pleaded with her mother once again and was turned down. Angry, the two got into a fight and Britt would call her boyfriend to come pick her up.

Brittanee decided to fool her mother. She told her mother that she wanted to stay at a friend's house nearby for a couple of days. Dawn reluctantly agreed but Brittanee headed off to South Carolina instead.

Dawn believed that someone had offered her something, like a "modeling job or some other kind of ruse" to get her to go down there. She had aspirations of being a model as well as getting into cosmetology. With her striking good looks, she would be a shoo-in for success in the modeling profession.

"Her biological father was Turkish," Dawn said. "She had a very European look."

Defying her mother, Brittanee would visit her boyfriend at his workplace and tried to entice him to come along. The young man declined, stating that he had to work.

Brittanee then left with her older friends Jennifer Oberer, Phillip Oberer and Allana Lippa to Myrtle Beach. Jennifer was twenty-one years old. Her brother Phillip would be charged with rape in an unrelated case (charges would be dropped) in 2010. It is believed that these were considered the 'cool kids' and that Britt wanted to hang out and be liked by them.

Britt texted her boyfriend numerous times throughout the trip, telling him about the ambience. She expressed her love for the hot weather, palm trees and the happy vibe of young people finally away from parental supervision. But according to friends and family, Brittanee didn't know the older kids that well.

She also called her mother and lied, telling her that she waswatching movies at a friend's house.

CHANGE OF HEART

Britt hit the clubs with her friends and her mood quickly changed. Her friends began using a lot of drugs and she didn't want any part of that scene. She went off by herself, checking out the local shops and walking down the beach.

She then met up with a friend from Rochester, a man named Peter Brozowitz. He was also in town and staying at the Blue Water Resort with his own group of friends; Matthew Abrams, Philip Watson, Keith Cummings, and Anthony Schimizzi. The 20-year old Brozowitz was a "club promoter" who got Brittanee into Club Kryptonite. The next morning, she would meet Peter again at the beach.

The next day, Brittanee called her younger sister and told her that she's at the beach. Her sister believed she's at the local beach which is only twenty-minutes away. Britt then has a friend to impersonate the parent of the friend get on the phone to talk to her mother. The friend assured Dawn that everything was okay.

Britt then got back on the phone with her mother.

"I'll see you tomorrow," Britt said. "I love you and I'll see you tomorrow."

It would be the last time Dawn would ever speak to her daughter.

THE MYSTERY OF WHAT HAPPENED THAT NIGHT

Brittanee decided she would meet up with her friend Peter that night. She borrowed a pair of shorts from a friend and headed out. She texted her boyfriend John, telling him that she's having a miserable time and that she doesn't like the people she went down with. Apparently, they were 'mean-girling' her after she didn't do drugs with them.

She then received a text from her friend who stated that she wants her shorts back. Irritated, Brittanee walked back to the hotel to return the item.

At least that is what her friends say happened as Britt would disappear into the night.

John then became worried when Britt did not text him back. He texted her a few more times, waited, received no answer then he threatened to tell her mother that she's in South Carolina if she doesn't respond back.

Convinced that something is wrong, John calls Dawn at home. He explained that Brittanee is in Myrtle Beach.

Dawn went livid but her anger soon turned to concern when Britt didn't respond to her own texts or calls.

Everyone in Brittanee's family was notified. Something was wrong. Terribly wrong.

The next morning Dawn, her parents and John all made the trek to Myrtle Beach to try and look for Brittanee.

THE SEARCH BEGINS

Police in Myrtle Beach were notified and questioned the friends that Britt had been staying with. Their answers were all the same, they had not seen Brittanee since last night. Police also turned to Dawn, questioning her about Brittanee's state of mind.

Would she run away? Had she done this before?

There was no indication that Brittanee had motivation to do such a thing. Nor did they have any reason to believe she was doing a lot of drinking or drugs.

With no other leads, detectives turned their eyes on the last person to have seen Brittanee, Peter Brozovitz.

Peter would make an appearance on the Dr.Phil show and proclaim his innocence. He stated that they were in his hotel room watching the Yankees-Red Sox game when Brittanee was engaged in a texting argument with Jen Oberer who wanted her shorts back.

He said she didn't have a problem with walking a mile back to her own hotel.

Brittanee's parents were on the show and berated Peter for not "being a gentleman" and driving her back to the hotel. They also found it suspicious that Peter and the rest of Brittanee's friends did not do more after she was missing.

"I had spoken with Peter that morning," Dawn said. "He was giving me three different scenarios...It's fishy."

Peter responded angrily, stating that he was 'being thrown under the bus.' The innuendos were clear, that even if he had nothing to do with Brittanee's disappearance, she went missing because he didn't look out for her.

What is suspicious is that Peter had abruptly left Myrtle Beach with his friends around 2 a.m, five hours after Brittanee had vanished. They left clothing behind in their hotel room and looked to have been in a rush.

Upon his return to Rochester, Peter hired a defense attorney.

Peter had told investigators that she left his room shortly upon arrival to return the pair of shorts to her friend. The detectives got a hold of the surveillance camera from the hotel and verified Peter's story. At precisely 8:48 that evening she was seen leaving Peter's hotel to return back to her own hotel. She should have shown up on a traffic camera about fifteen minutes away but she never made it that far. She was abducted somewhere along that street.

Police continued to question Peter. The young man stated that one of his friends was told by his mother to return home immediately. This story was corroborated and law enforcement did not pursue the matter any further.

Instead, they now focused on Britt's cell phone.

Britt's last text message to her boyfriend was around 8:58. Ten minutes after she had left the hotel she texted "I'm packing and going to sleep probably."

This would be the last outbound message she sent as then John began texting her repeatedly with no answer back.

But the calls she received from John and her friends were pinged by her cell phone. Every time a friend called, her cell phone communicated with the nearest tower.

In looking at her cell phone records, she was moving southbound. The last ping was received at the Poleyard boat landing.

Fifty miles away from Myrtle Beach and two counties over.

Whoever abducted Brittanee knew exactly where they were going. The place was isolated, a rural country islet that only fishermen or locals would know about.

This was not the kind of place a seventeen-year-old girl would go to on Spring Break.

The investigators launched their search in the area that was about four miles in radius. Unfortunately, the terrain was treacherous. Alligators, wild hogs, snakes and biting insects the size of golf balls populated the area looking for their next meal.

Four-wheelers were brought in to keep the alligators away from the sniffing cadaver dogs. Investigators came to the site armed to shoot any wild hogs that came near.

"If her body is here," one investigator told Dawn in an ominous tone. "She would be eaten within six hours."

The search was frantic in the beginning but investigators seemed to lose hope after a few days passed. Britt's family returned home to Rochester with sunken hearts.

Brittanee's little brother chastized her friend upon their returning, stating "I thought you were bringing Brittanee back!"

Eight months later, police still had no promising leads. They would get an anonymous tip to check out an area a few miles north of the original search area near the Scantee River.

Once again, they came up with nothing. But a couple out fishing found a pair of sunglasses that looked as if they would belong to a teenage girl.

Neither her parents nor her boyfriend recognized the sunglasses as belonging to Brittanee. A DNA test was performed on the glasses and nothing was found.

Her mother continued to believe that she's alive.

"I think she was taken and held against her well," Dawn said. "I think she has become the victim of human trafficking."

Investigators and reporters shot down the notion, however. Typically, human trafficking occurs where the victim has a language barrier and Myrtle Beach was not exactly a hot bed for that type of crime. The police did not rule it out but it is low on their list of possibilities.

From 1997 to 2010, South Carolina has reported 12 cases of documented sex tracking. All were women, according to Doors to Freedom, an organization that helps victims of sex trafficking.

A few months later, police would receive some cell phone footage of Brittanee shot by a young man she had met. There were a group of teens antagonizing her and she wanted the young man's help to hang out with her so they would stop. He shot some footage of her sitting by herself, texting her boyfriend. He has since been cleared of any suspicion as he did have an alibi.

Pressed for suspects, law enforcement looked at every possible lead.

Three years later, authorities identified fifty-one year old Raymond Moody as a person of interest. They obtained a search warrant for a Georgetown motel room where Moody rented out at the time of Brittanee's disappearance. They noted that Moody had received a traffic ticket in Surfside beach just one day after Brittanee went missing.

Moody was a a registered sex offender, having raped a nine-year old girl in 1983. He was released in June of 2004. But Moody did not cooperate with investigators and remained tight-lipped under interrogation.

He is also a suspect in the case of Crystal Soles who disappeared in January of 2005.

"We've heard his name before," Dawn Drexel said. "It's a possibility the cases are connected. We don't know what happened to Crystal or Brittanee."

Moody lived in an area where Brittanee's cell phone last pinged. He was referred to as "Mr.Clean" because of his resemblance to the bald character in the Mr. Clean commercials. He has not been mentioned in any police reports since 2012, however.

The FBI would get involved and offer their belief that Brittanee was abducted and taken to a "stash house" where she was raped and then murdered. Her body was then wrapped in plastic and she was thrown into an alligator pit where her body would presumably be eaten.

This narrative was offered by FBI Agent Gerrick Munoz who obtained the informaton from an inmate named Taquan Brown. Brown is serving a 25-year sentence for a different case but stated he was present during Britt's last moments.

He said he had seen Britt when he visited a "stash house" which was a moniker used by drug dealers to describe a place where they stashed weapons, money or drugs.

Brown stated that Taylor picked Britt up in Myrtle Beach and took her to McClellanville. Once there he "showed her off, introduced her to some other friend that were there...they ended up tricking her out with some of their friends, offering her to them and getting a human trafficking situation."

The stash house was in the McClellanville area, the last location where Britt's cell phone was pinged.

Brown told the officials that he saw Da'Shaun Taylor, who was 16 years old at the time, and several other men "sexually abusing Brittanee Drexel."

Brown then claimed he went to the backyard to give Da'Shaun's father money.

During this time, Britt tried to escape. She was caught by one of the men who "pistol whipped" her across the head. She was then taken back inside the house.

Brown stated that he heard two gunshots and then saw the woman being wrapped up and removed from the home.

The FBI agent revealed that "several witnesses" have told him that she was dumped in a pond that was filled with alligators.

Taylor has since been convicted of robbery in 2011 and could face a life sentence. He stated that he knows nothing of Britt's case and with the lack of evidence he has not faced any charges in her disappearance.

Chad Drexel, however, thinks Taylor may have been involved.

He recalled a time when he was out handing out Brittanee's missing person fliers and handed it to Taylor who was in his car.

"I gave him the flier," Chad said. "He had a car full of brothers, friends. He handed the flier to one guy in the back seat. They all laughed and then drove away and threw the flier out the window."

"I got mad. I said 'There's something about this guy...'"

After the information was released to the public, Taylor's mother, Reverend Joanne Taylor, immediately defended her son.

She stated that he had already served his time for the robbery (a McDonald's restaurant) and that he was a "great kid" that was only

16 years old at the time of Brittanee's disappearance. During her son's hearing, Taylor's mother took the stand and said the following:

"And I want to say that at the time of this alleged abduction, he was 16 years old. I was never a mother thatwould let my kids run loosely, and definitely not with the father, you know, out to do things. I kept great hold on him. I am a pastor of a church. They were in church, they had a strict bedtime, I knew every place that they went. MyrtleBeach would not be a place that he would go at the age of 16. So I just, you know, I ask for your fairness, I ask for, you know, the correct justice in this case. And know that he is not a flight risk. I mean, I teached them good values, I instill in them what few things that have happened, they have exemplified overall what I've taught them. He is not, you know, a flight risk or anything.

Chad Drexel read the testimony and immediately took to his own Facebook page.

> *I would like to set the record STRAIGHT with a STRONG REPLY to Joan Taylor's comments to the Post Courier in South Carolina this past Friday.*

> *Based on evidence the FBI and the Myrtle Beach Police department has gathered, along with FACTS and SPECIFIC INFORMATION gathered from a team of Private Investigators that I HIRED to work with local law enforcement actively during the case (which will SOON COME TO LIGHT) – we have no doubt Timothy Da'Shaun Taylor played a significant role in the abduction and murder of my daughter.*

> *Of course the mother of Timothy Da'Shaun Taylor is going to defend her son – as a father I can understand a need to defend your children. What I DON'T understand is defending your children when you must KNOW the truth.*

Her assumptions and words stated have been verified INCORRECT and couldn't be farther from the TRUTH. We know Timothy Da'Shaun Taylor was witnessed by others (Witnesses NOT IN JAIL) with my daughter – we are just praying that they do the RIGHT thing and stop forward with what they know. Additionally he has been seen and followed to the EXACT area where my daughter's DNA was found. Joan Taylor claimed that the FBI and government are falsely accusing her son because of witnesses IN JAIL?! Well, we have other specific evidence, that I can NOT disclose at this time for the safety of my daughters case, which corroborates these testimonies!! Timothy Da'Shaun Taylor is KNOWN to be involved in dog fighting, bringing drugs to parties, and raping women (mostly Caucasian young women) he either picks up UNWILLINGLY or friends of friends that end up being drugged and taken there. This IS ONLY THE BEGINNING!! There is a TON more "EVIDENCE and HORRIBLE INFO" we would like the PUBLIC in that area be aware of for their safety, but we are unable to disclose at this time.

WITHOUT A DOUBT ....Timothy Da'Shaun Taylor is a suspect in my daughter's Disappearance and Murder! My family and I will be following the FBI's requests to keep specific details in our daughter's case under wrap until THIS HORRIBLE PIECE OF TRASH goes to Prison for Life. After the guilty verdict, we will be happy to dispel these fairy tales that are being spun by Timothy's family. It is disgraceful the way this FAMILY and their FRIENDS are supporting and claiming innocence of a "PROVEN"

FELON without even looking at the evidence presented and the FACTS surrounding the case.

Also adding this PIECE OF TRASH photo so everyone can see WHO HE IS!

On March 25th, 2017, FBI agents called Dawn Drexel to inform her they may have located Brittanee's remains. They are now searching an area 45 miles north of their previous search spot.

After two days, however, they gave up the search.

The case is ongoing.

MISSING LAUREN

MEGAN FAIRCHILD

The Unsolved Disappearance of Lauren Spierer

Lauren Spierer was a 20-year college student at Indiana University at the time of her disappearance in June 2011. Her disappearance, subsequent police manhunt and investigation, generated widespread coverage in the national news. There has been tons of speculation and gossip as to what happened that night and the notable reluctance of the Bloomington Police Department to release further footage of the surveillance cameras of her walking outside the bar. But what remains most haunting about the case is Lauren herself. A bright and beautiful young woman, her smile captured the hearts of everyone who met her and everyone who saw her face on her missing posters. Lauren's Spierer's disappearance remains one of the most well-known unsolved mysteries in modern U.S. History.

This is what happened that night...

Who Was Lauren Spierer?

Lauren Spierer was born in Scarsdale, New York in January 1991 to Robert Spierer and Charlene Spierer. She was raised in the Scarsdale, a small town of just over 17,000 people, located in Westchester County and a short train ride from New York City.

"In all of her family videos," forensic psychologist Paul Jones said. "Lauren is shown to be a vivacious young lady with a zest for life. She sings and dances and mugs for the camera. She obviously came from a loving home."

Lauren would graduate from Edgemont High School in 2009 and moved to Indiana that year to begin studying for a bachelor's degree in textiles and merchandising.

Spierer enrolled at Indiana University along with a close circle of friends and her boyfriend, Jesse Wolff. Lauren met Jesse during her childhood at Camp Towanda, a summer camp for teenagers in Pennsylvania. While Lauren was a strong student, she was arrested for public intoxication roughly nine months before she disappeared.

"I don't think I realized to what degree, you know?" Lauren's mother said. "It was a little bit of a shock."

Shortly after completing her finals in the spring semester of her sophomore year, Lauren went out for a night of partying with friends. She would never be seen again.

The Night of the Disappearance

Lauren set out to her friend's house on the night of June 3rd, 2011 for a night of partying at a local sports bar. She left her apartment at the Smallwood Plaza apartment complex with her friend David Rohn, traveling to their mutual friend Jay Rosenbaum's house before heading out to the bar. While at Rosenbaum's house, Spierer and Rohn begin drinking and "pre-gaming" with Rosenbaum's neighbor, Cory Rossman. The three students spent nearly an hour drinking before heading to Kilroy's Sports Bar shortly after 1:30am.

"Kilroy's was 'the' hangout near the campus," Jones said. "It was a crowded place not only inside but outside as well with tons of college students just milling about. It would be easy to get lost in the shuffle with all the people that are there. Too easy for a predator, if there was one, to target a victim and wait for her to separate from the pack."

Witnesses who were present at the bar describe Lauren and her friends as very intoxicated and she is reported as having fallen down several times while out partying. The friends spent a little less than hour at the sports bar before Lauren and Rossman are spotted leaving the bar and heading to her apartment complex. Lauren's shoes and cell phone are later found at the bar, and she is seen walking barefoot down the street, heavily intoxicated, by a concerned passerby.

Surveillance cameras would show Lauren entering her apartment complex minutes after leaving the nearby sports bar, but she would be seen leaving her apartment and stumbling into a nearby alley minutes after.

Brad Garrett, a former FBI agent who assisted 20/20 with their investigation into Lauren's disappearance claims that Rossman got into a physical confrontation with several of her neighbors, leading to their departure from her apartment complex. Garrett said, "Apparently they don't like the way [Rossman] is handling Lauren. And Rossman supposedly said something smart to him and this guy decides to deck him."

She and Rossman then walked over to Rossman's apartment, where Rossman vomited on his way up the stairs. Rossman's roommate, Michael Beth, would later report that both friends were visibly intoxicated, stumbling and slurring their words. Beth soon helped Rossman get to bed and offered Lauren a place to stay for the night. Lauren declined and headed next door to her close friend Jay Rosenbaum's apartment before heading back to her apartment. She was last seen walking south on College Avenue, near the intersection of College Avenue and 11th Street.

Later that morning, Lauren's boyfriend, Jesse Wolff, texted Lauren to ask how she was doing. After receiving a reply from a staff member of Kilroy's Sports Bar stating that her phone was left at the bar, Wolff reported her as missing to the local police department.

Police Timeline

12:30am – Spierer is spotted leaving her apartment with her close friend David Rohn. The two meet up with Cory Rossman, the neighbor of their mutual friend Jay Rosenbaum.

1:46am – Spierer is spotted entering Kilroy's Sports Bar. It is later reported that Spierer used a fake ID to get into the bar.

2:37am – Witnesses see Lauren leave the sports bar with Cory Rossman. Spierer left her shoes and cell phone at the bar. The pair set off to Spierer's apartment.

2:30am – Witnesses see Spierer enter her apartment complex, Smallwood Plaza. A man named Zach Oakes, whiling walking past Spierer, notices that she is severely intoxicated and asks if she is "okay."

2:48am – Spierer is spotted by security cameras leaving her apartment and entering an alley located between College Avenue and

Morton Street. She did not enter her apartment or put a new pair of shoes on.

2:51am – Security cameras capture Lauren and Rossman leaving the alley and walking towards an empty parking lot. Police would later find Spierer's keys and wallet lying on the ground in the vicinity of her path.

3:00am – Lauren and Rossman arrive at Rossman's apartment. Rossman's roommate, Michael Beth, reported that both friends were heavily intoxicated and having difficulties walking. Rossman was spotted vomiting on the way upstairs. Beth reported that he helped Rossman to bed and encouraged Spierer to spend the night until she could sober up, but Spierer declined.

3:30am – Beth called his neighbor and Spierer's friend Jay Rosenbaum to enlist his help in taking care of Spierer. Lauren goes to Rosenbaum's apartment and used his phone to place two calls before leaving his apartment.

3:38am – A local bar manager later says that he saw a man pick up a woman matching Lauren's description and sling her over his shoulder near 10th Street and College Avenue. There is no video evidence to support this assertion, but a private investigator hired by the Spierer's later says that he believes this was Lauren, but that the bar manager's recollection of the time this happened was incorrect.

4:30am – Rosenbaum states that Lauren left his apartment, purportedly to return to her own apartment. He states that he last saw her walking south along College Avenue, near the corner of College Avenue and 11th Street. She was described as wearing black leggings and a white shirt, and barefoot.

4:35am – There are reports that a homeless man hears a woman scream for help near where Spierer was last seen. Investigators have been unable to confirm this rumor, but a local homeless man, Franklin "Road Dog" Crawford, who may have been the man in question died just days after Lauren's disappearance.

4:30pm – Friends of Lauren report her as missing to the local Bloomington Police Department. Lauren's sister, Rebecca, calls Robert and Charlene Spierer to tell them that Lauren has been reported as missing. They call Lauren's boyfriend, Jesse Wolff, who is at the Bloomington police station when he receives the call.

Police Investigation

Police conducted a nine-day search of the areas near her apartment, including the Sycamore Ridge Landfill located in Pimento, Indiana. They were joined by Lauren's parents, the Bloomington Police Department, the Indiana University Police Department, FBI, and hundreds of volunteers, searching the abandoned landfill, local forests, and quarries. However, their extensive search would ultimately prove fruitless. Although the authorities received hundreds of tips related to her disappearance, none of the leads led to any answers.

"The search would be an emotionally brutal time for Lauren's parents," Jones said. "They would have to go through the agony of walking through creeks and quarries shouting out their daughter's name to no avail. The father said that the worst time was when they witnessed the city bulldozer sift through the nearby landfill. Combing through the garbage, looking for their daughter. The pain they experienced is simply unimaginable."

Drug Use the Night of the Disappearance

Former FBI investigator and 20/20 researcher Brad Garrett has stated that he believes drugs played a part in her disappearance that night, stating that they had role "either in her own demise or because it placed her in harm's way because she was so impaired." In addition, both Lauren's boyfriend and her friends told police officers that she used both drugs and alcohol on a regular basis leading up to her disappearance. Officers would later find "a small amount of cocaine" during a search of her apartment and Lauren's parents would later reveal that she was arrested for public intoxication and underage consumption of alcohol approximately nine months before her disappearance.

Nadine Wolff, the mother of Lauren's boyfriend Jesse Wolff, would later claim that Lauren was kicked out of the summer camp where she met Jesse and her core group of friends in high school because of drug use.

"This poor little girl is not with us today because of her drug abuse," Nadine said.

For their part, Lauren's parents would later respond in the press that "We are appalled that the Wolff's have defamed our daughter knowing that Lauren will never have the opportunity to respond."

Rosenbaum would corroborate these claims of drug use that night, telling authorities that Lauren snorted Klonopin and cocaine that evening, in addition to drinking a large amount of alcohol. Her family would also disclose that Lauren suffered from a rare heart condition, long QT syndrome, which may have been a contributing factor.

While police have stated that this may be a case of her friends disposing of her body to hide her overdose in their presence, they have also stated that this may be a case of abduction. A private investigator later hired by the Spierer's would similarly express doubt that this may have simply been a case of students panicking after Lauren suffered an overdose.

Parents' Public Statements

Lauren's parents have publicly said that they believe Lauren is dead. Robert Spierer has speculated that, given Lauren's erratic behavior the night of her disappearance and extreme level of intoxication, she may have been drugged while at the bar.

"One of her friends stated that it wouldn't be out of the ordinary for her to take off her shoes at the bar," Jones said. "They would have beach sand inside the bar to add to the party atmosphere. As far as leaving her cell phone there, she may have just been completely out of it and forgot it."

Lauren's parents have also stated that they believe the young men Lauren partied with that night, and possibly her boyfriend, know more about her disappearance than they have let on. They base these accusations on the fact that all of the men involved refused to take a polygraph test and hired lawyers shortly after Lauren's disappearance.

Suspects

Her Group of Friends

Brad Garrett, the former FBI agent hired by Lauren's parents to investigate her disappearance, stated that the first suspects in her disappearance were her friends. He said, "When something happens to someone, it's usually from their own circle." Robert Spierer, Lauren's father, has noted on several occasions that the young men with Lauren the night of her disappearance, sought legal representation "very early on," which he claims created a "wall of access" that prevented the family from learning more about their daughter's last hours.

In addition, while Lauren's boyfriend, Jesse Wolff, was very helpful in the beginning of the investigation and cooperated fully with the police, her father notes that Wolff's parents brought him home to New York shortly after Lauren's disappearance, saying "I thought it was odd." It should be noted that Wolff was never spotted outside of his apartment the night of Lauren's disappearance, and he says that he was at home watching the NBA finals while she was out drinking. Wolff's roommate says that Wolff was in bed by 2:30am, hours before Lauren was last seen.

Despite Wolff's alibi and statements from Lauren's friends describing Wolff as "the most loving boyfriend" who would never harm Lauren, the Spierer's are still unsure of Wolff's potential involvement. Brad Garrett told 20/20 that he's "not comfortable that [he] actually knows what he was doing in the early morning hours of June 3."

Cory Rossman, who had only recently met Lauren and spent most of the night with her the night of her disappearance, provided a DNA sample to the police early in their investigation and has maintained his innocence. However, Rossman has refused to speak with the Spierers or their private investigators, claiming to have lost his memory after being punched in Lauren's apartment complex. Robert Spierer has noted that he is skeptical of Rossman's statements, saying "I'm not sure of anything, but what I do know is that there's been a complete lack of cooperation. And he was the person who spent the most time with Lauren in the last hours of her being seen."

While Rossman seldom speaks with reporters about the case, he told the press in 2011 that "I was not the last person with her and that's all I can say, I'm sorry. But I just hope they find her as soon as possible and I am praying for her and her family."

"If we're to judge who looks the most suspicious," Jones said. "My bet is on Rossman. His mug shot is certainly suggestive of someone who is angry and secretive. Out of all the persons of interests he has behaved as if he is either guilty or knows a lot more than he has revealed."

The White Pickup Truck

Another well-known scenario is that Lauren was abducted by a stranger who was driving around Bloomington the night of her disappearance, and who may have viewed a visibly intoxicated, stumbling, and shoeless Lauren as an ideal target. Police have stated that surveillance footage from nearby businesses show a white pickup truck driving around the area where Lauren was last seen. A local police official would say that it is "absolutely" possible that this truck may have been involved in Lauren's disappearance.

Brad Garrett, the investigator hired by Lauren's parents, has theorized that James McClish, a felon was recently released from prison at the time of Lauren's disappearance, may have been involved. He was released from prison after being convicted of assaulting his ex-wife and reportedly drove a white pickup truck at this time. He was living in a halfway house for recently released convicts just minutes away from where Lauren was last seen. Garrett says that her abduction "could have taken 10 seconds. At that point he's got her and he takes her to wherever."

During the course of Garrett's investigation, he says that a woman who knew McClish telephoned him and told him, "You need to check him out. He was there. He's made comments, 'You know what happened to her [Lauren], the same thing could happen to you." She also claimed that McClish murdered Lauren and buried her body on a farm.

However, McClish was approached about this claim by 20/20 and he agreed to take a lie detector test, administered by a former NYPD detective and polygraph examiner, Ralph Nieves. After administering the test, Nieves said that McClish was telling the truth and was not involved in Lauren's disappearance. After finishing the test, McClish told the investigators "I wish you guys the best of luck. I do."

A Lead from Jail

In 2012, another student at Indiana University, Corey Hamersley, was arrested after suffering a mental breakdown while high on drugs and after shooting at local police officers. Hamersley was reportedly heavily involved in the drug culture at Indiana University and was a former star athlete for the university.

Shortly after being sentenced to 24 years in prison for firing at police officers, an inmate in the same cell block as Hamersley claims that Hamersley said of Lauren's disappearance, "I knew the guy that did that."

"This is one of those jailhouse confessions," Jones said. "We really don't know if it has credibility or not but the inmate stated that Hamersley told him that Lauren overdosed on ecstasy. She passed out and they didn't know what to do with her so they drove her down to the Ohio River and dumped her body there. Far fetched for any normal human being to do something like that. The normal response would be to call 911. But these are drunk college students from privileged backgrounds. They do not want anything on their record that would mar their futures."

Brad Garrett says he believes that there could be some truth to this story, "Because the idea is very simple. One of the mistakes in most criminal cases is we, investigators, try to make them too complicated... The simplest is, she dies at a party in Bloomington and somebody got rid of her." This theory on Lauren's disappearance is even more compelling when you consider that Lauren suffered from a heart condition that could have led to an overdose or adverse reaction.

For his part, Hamersley denies any involvement in Lauren's disappearance, and has stated "absolutely" did not help move her body, and that "I do not want to be associated with this at all."

Civil Lawsuit

Robert and Charlene Spierer filed a civil lawsuit against the three young men who were with Lauren the night of her disappearance, Cory Rossman, Jay Rosenbaum, and Michael Beth. Lauren's parents claimed that the three men were negligent in their care of Lauren the night of her disappearance, and that both Rossman and Rosenbaum provided Lauren with alcohol throughout the night despite the fact that she was "visibly intoxicated."

Despite the fact that none of the men have been publicly named as suspects by the local police department, Charlene Spierer publicly said, "I truly don't think it was a random abduction, I think that somebody Lauren knew was responsible for the events of that evening."

Eventually, the civil lawsuit against each of the young men would be dismissed. In their suit against Michael Beth, Robert and Lauren Spierer claimed that he had assumed a "duty of care" for Lauren when she arrived at his apartment visibly intoxicated and he offered to allow her to stay the night. The federal judge presiding over the case, Tanya Pratt, dismissed the case against Beth in 2013, saying that he had no duty to care for Lauren Spierer, despite her level of intoxication.

Judge Pratt would then dismiss the Spierer's case against Cory Rossman and Jay Rosenbaum in 2014, saying that, "Unfortunately, there could be any number of theories as to what happened to Lauren and what, if any, injuries she may have sustained. Without evidence to provide these theories, it would be impossible for a jury to determine if whatever happened to Spierer was a natural and probable cause of her intoxication, without any other intervening acts that would break the causal chain."

Robert and Charlene Spierer maintain that the three young men were involved in the disappearance of Lauren and have appealed the dismissal of their civil suits. They have also hired private investigators to look into the three men's possible role in their daughter's disappearance, and have publicly claimed that the men have been less than cooperative with the family and the police throughout the process. Ron Chapman, the attorney for Michael Beth and David Rohn, countered, "They've been interviewed and interviewed and interviewed, and to say they've been less than forthcoming is just not accurate."

Recent Developments

The Bloomington Police Department publicly stated that Lauren's disappearance may be related to the abduction and murder of another IU student, Hannah Wilson. Wilson was also partying at Kilroy's Sports Bar the night of her disappearance on April 24, 2015, before leaving the bar in a taxi.

Wilson's body was found the next day in Brown County, Indiana, and her murder was investigated as a possible link to Spierer's case. However, despite the arrest of a local man, Daniel Messel, in Wilson's murder, a private investigator hired by the Spierer's determined that the two cases were unrelated.

In January 2016, the FBI and local police department began to investigate a property belonging to the family of Justin Wagers, a registered sex offender, who police believe may have been involved in Lauren's disappearance.

"Wagers was a serial flasher," Jones said. "He'd yell 'Hey Lady!' at women and expose himself, getting arrested numerous times. His behavior did escalate, however, and he did work for an excavation company so he would know how to hide a body. But his involvement is pure speculation. For the most part, flashers are different animals than a kidnapping rapist."

The house, located in the 2900 block of Old Morgantown Road in Martinsville, Indiana, was searched by officers with cadaver dogs. The dogs got a "hit" on the site, which caused a team of forensic investigators to dig up parts of the property in search of evidence related to Lauren's disappearance, but no definitive evidence was found.

Lauren's case remains open and although the case has been "reinvigorated" the mystery of her disappearance seems no more closer to being solved than the night she vanished.

MISTY COPSEY

LORI DUNLAP

Misty Copsey was fourteen years old when she disappeared on September 17th, 1992 after a trip to the Puyallup Fair.

Her case remains a showcase of administrative screw-ups and dropped balls. She was initially thought of as a runaway before foul play was finally suspected a month after the fact. Subsequently, there have been at least five people suspected of committing her abduction.

But the Puyallup police did not get within sniffing distance of Misty or charging anyone with her disappearance. Three different police chiefs and numerous detectives all took a swing at the case and whiffed. No one in law enforcement has been able to answer the question on everyone's lips.

What happened to Misty Copsey?

A GOOD GIRL

Misty was born in 1978 to Diana and Paul "Buck" Copsey. Her father was a firefighter but the couple split up shortly after she was born and Misty lived with her mother.

Misty got good grades in school, excelling particularly in Math. During her last quarter at Spanaway Lake Junior High School, she got A's and B's. Athletic, she played softball, volleyball, and basketball before breaking both forearms during an athletic practice.

Misty was not the ringleader of a bad crowd. She was diffident but funny, entertaining her friends while skipping around and singing the theme song to Sesame Street.

She did not have much in regards to material wants. Her mother eked out a living as an in-home care nurse and they lived in a mobile home park until she was fourteen. Seeking a better place to live, Diana and Misty moved into a duplex where she now had her own room. But Misty longed for her friend who lived in and around the old trailer park. She would make it back there when she could to just hang out.

Tall, blonde and with green eyes, Misty was cute enough to draw the attention of boys. She remained chaste, however, and was not dating like so many of her other friends.

Her innocent, girl-next-door looks would draw the attention of Rheuban Schmidt. Rheuban looked like a casting call actor for a meth head. He sported a reverse mullet, a hairstyle that was cut close to the sides with curls on top. He had beady, green eyes that screamed low IQ. One of Misty's friends described him as a "scuzzy looking dude" but he nonetheless befriends Misty, much to the chagrin of her mother.

Diana grew suspicious of the relationship as Rheuban was four years older and a high school dropout. On one occasion, she listened in on the other end of a phone conversation Misty was having with Rheuban.

"I get horny just looking at you, Misty," Rheuban said, whispering like an old pervert.

Diana became enraged and ordered her daughter off the phone.

"Don't ever talk to that idiot again...."

ENTER CORY BOBER

Cory Bober was a thorn in the side of police every since the Green River killings became a national news story. He would insist that the police are "incompetent fools" while organizing his own searches for her remains. Diana would later accuse him of killing her daughter but he would respond by telling Diana that she was being "ungrateful." He was, after all, the only man on the case.

Bober was a recluse without a vehicle or a drive's license. An inveterate marijuana user, he had a record for both possession and dealing. He was also obsessed with cases of murdered or slain women in his home state of Washington. He had a stack of binders with autopsy reports, pictures, and other arcane details.

Bober came under the radar of the police in Puyallup when he became obsessed with the Green River Killer case. He had a brief acquaintance with Randall Dean Achziger, remembering a conversation where the man told him that the killer inserted rocks into the remains of his victim. Bober became suspicious as that would turn out to be a piece of information only known to police. He then went on a one-man crusade to prove the guilt of Achziger. Bober would interview his ex-girlfriends, friends, co-workers and present all of this in an affidavit to the courts.

Achziger found it ridiculous and annoying.

So did the police.

The Green River Killer would turn out to be a painter named Gary Leon Ridgway.

Bober didn't give up, however. He knew Achziger was the guy.

Bober had his own theories about who was performing the killings. Some were wild and outlandish conspiracy theories. Others were spot on. He would notice that there were victims that "had disappeared on the very same date that others were discovered. Some victims seemed to almost 'commemorate' the deaths or discoveries of others; one would die on a particular date and another would disappear a year to the day later on the very same date."

The police dismissed his theories as the rantings of a crack head. But Bober would be willing to show the proof of his connect the dots calculations. He pointed to the cases of Kim Delange, a 15-year-old killed in 1988 and Anna Chebetnoy, a 14-year-old killed in 1990. Both of their bodies would be found along Highway 410, east of Enumclaw.

Bober discovered that the remains of both girls were found in the same section of 410. The girls were found two years and one month apart. He felt that the killer was following a pattern.

He called the police department and left a voice mail. He predicted that a teen girl from Puyallup would disappear and her remains would be found on Highway 410 in the same vicinity where the other girl's bodies were found. Bober gave him the name of the man whom he felt was the serial killer.

Randall Achziger.

But the police were now used to his calls and viewed him as a crank. A nutcake with a strange vendetta.

His prediction would be half-right, however.

There would be no body found on Highway 410.

But a teenage girl would disappear.

Her name was Misty Copsey.

A NIGHT AT THE FAIR

On September 17th, 1992, Diana told her daughter Misty and her best friend Trina Bevard to behave themselves. Misty had convinced her mother to let them stay out that night...free of any meddlesome adults. But Trina's guardian would not allow her to go without an adult driving them home.

Diana worked as a caregiver for a 97-year-old Alzheimer patient who could not be left alone. She would not be able to drive the girls home. But Misty checked the bus schedules and convinced her mother that they would be okay. There was a bus that left the fair at 8:40 p.m.

Misty then convinced her mother to lie to Trina's guardian, Marlene Shoemaker.

"No worries," Diana said to Marlene. "I'll bring them home."

She wanted to be the cool parent, different from the stuffy adults who forgot what it was like to be fourteen. If it meant telling a white lie so her little girl could have some happiness, so be it.

What was the worst that could happen?

Diana dropped the girls off and gave them one last warning.

"Get home safe."

It would be the last time she would ever see her daughter again.

THE PHONE CALL

A few hours later, Diana would then receive a phone call from Misty as she tended to her elderly patient. Misty told her that she had missed the bus but could get a ride from Rheuban Schmidt.

Diana, knowing what kind of unsavory character Schmidt was, adamantly refused. She told Misty to find someone else to give her a ride back. Misty had an electronic diary which she used to store phone numbers. She told her mother she would find someone trustworthy to call for a ride.

"You call me back when you find someone," Diana said.

"I will. I promise."

Diana would wait all night for the phone call.

In the ensuing hours, Misty would not call back.

Worried, Diane called home in the hope that Misty had gotten a ride without calling her.

No answer.

Diana didn't panic. She figured that Misty went home with that scumbag Schmidt and didn't want to get yelled out for disobeying her.

She's going to get yelled at either/or. All Diana wanted was for her daughter to be safe.

Her shift finally ended and Diana drove back home in a rush.

Upon entering her house, she called out for Misty.

Silence.

She went into Misty's room and saw that it had been untouched from the previous night.

Diana would call the police in a panic. She told them that her daughter had not come home from the fair. The dispatcher would tell her that the police could not do anything about it for thirty days as it "sounded like a runaway case."

Diana knew otherwise.

Trying to calm herself, she figured that Misty was with Trina, that the two of them would be okay.

She called Trina's home.

No answer.

She then began scorching the earth with phone calls.

She would call Rheuban but he told her that she called but he didn't have the gas to go get her. She then called numerous friends of Misty and her mother.

No one had seen Misty.

She called Trina's home again, got no answer, then drove out to her house. She then went to the police department and filed a formal report with the Pierce County's Sheriff's Department who handled runaways as opposed to the Puyallup Police.

MISTY'S MISSING

Misty's friend Trina called Diana after she came back from school. She told the frantic mother that she didn't know where Misty was.

"The last time I saw her, she was heading for the bus," she said.

Diana would call Rheuban again. She would get his roommate this time, James Tinsley.

Diana needed answers. She interrogated the young fifteen-year-old like a grizzled police detective. She asked if Rheuban had been home all night. James then told her that Rheuban and his uncle went to pick up Misty but that he wasn't home just yet.

Later, Diana would call back and Rheuban would tell her that his roommate got the story wrong. He went to a party instead and didn't pick up Misty. He didn't know where she was.

Diana pleaded for the police to do something. They dragged their heels and began talking to some of Misty's friends. "Just call if she calls," they informed them. "No one gets in trouble."

Diana printed fliers with Misty's picture. She plastered them in and around the fairgrounds while calling the media.

The one woman search team would yield no leads. Rheuban would stop by and ask if the police had found anything yet. Diana would then wait at the bus stop near the fairgrounds to inquire with different drivers on the route. She found one driver who said that he saw Misty. She had asked when the next bus to Spanaway was arriving. The driver said it wasn't and that he was done for the night. He gave her instructions on which bus to take but she walked away before he could complete his sentence.

AN ERROR OF JUDGEMENT

Among the many mistakes that the Puyallup police made in the investigation of Misty's disappearance was to make the assumption that she was a runaway. Why they didn't entertain the prospect that she could have been kidnapped and murdered gave the abductor precious time to cover his tracks.

The police came to this erroneous conclusion after they interviewed Misty's mother, Diana. They thought she was a liar and an alcoholic. They then interviewed a pair of Misty's classmates who really didn't know her that well or accompany her to the fair.

A series of cover-ups then ensued, as the police told the media Misty had been found (where they got that information remains a mystery) and made no further investigation.

Until Diana and the media started to make a fuss. The department had to save face and eventually one of the detectives believed that this was not a runaway case.

Misty's disappearance could not be ignored any longer.

Police would talk to the various fair workers and security guards. No one had recalled seeing Misty.

The police then turned to her family, interviewing and doing background checks on both Misty's father, Buck, and Diana.

Their impressions of the duo would support their initial theory that Misty runaway. Diana was an alcoholic with multiple DUIs and seven years prior she had been convicted of welfare fraud. Buck confirmed that his daughter and Diana would have their issues.

Carver then discovered that Diana had filed a runaway report on Misty a month prior to her disappearing.

Diana would later state that the report was wrong. She thought Misty had disappeared then found her in the bedroom. She was too ashamed to tell the police it had been a false alarm.

With the police questioning and media coverage, Misty Copsey was now the talk of her Spanaway Lake Junior High school.

Rumors would abound at the school, one of which came from Misty Matthews who said that Misty had called her from Olympia. Another student stated that she saw Misty at a Color Me Badd concert at the fair.

The rumors were enough to prompt Carver to remove Misty from the FBI's National Crime Information Center as a missing person. He would once again treat her as a runaway.

BOBER'S THEORY

Cory Bober's knew he was right. He knew that police would find a body of a young woman off Highway 410.

He waited but nothing happened.

Until his mother showed him the flier of Misty's disappearance.

Right again!

Heart racing, he called the number on the flier. Bober would get into contact with Diana and hurriedly told her all about his research.

He talked about the Green River Killer, where and how he killed his victims. He would tell Diana that her disappearance was connected to the same guy responsible for the murdered Puyallup Girls, Kim Delange and Anne Chebetnoy.

Cory would apologize to Diana because he knew that Misty was dead. He predicted her body would be found somewhere along Highway 410.

The two would form an uneasy alliance. Bober became Misty's personal avenger. He would start a phone/letter/media campaign to prove the police wrong and himself right.

Misty was no runaway.

She was a victim of Randall Achziger.

In October, however, Bober would be arrested for selling marijuana. He was then accosted by Sgt.Herm Carver who tired of the young man meddling in police affairs.

"He walked in the room I was being held in – looking tired and pissed off. He said, 'I got out of bed tonight, and came down here to meet you – just to see what kind of a hypocrite you REALLY ARE!'

I said (being cocky), 'It's not MY FAULT – HERM – that you don't believe Misty Copsey's MISSING!!'

He yelled (angry), 'DON'T YOU EVER CALL ME BY MY FIRST NAME – IT'S SGT. CARVER TO YOU!!!'"

Bober's journals, November 1992

THIRTY DAYS MISSING

Sgt. Herm Carver and Deputy Brian Coburn would each individually warn Diana of the troublemaker that Bober was. Still, the worried mother would welcome his assistance as she needed all the help she could get. After numerous phone calls, the two would finally meet after a month of Misty being missing. Diana had nowhere else to turn but to the shaggy-haired twenty-six-year-old who lived with his parents.

The police were going through the motions on their end. Carver reactivated Misty's name on state and national lists but only because he was legally required to do so. At this point, he still believed Misty to be a runaway and doubted Diana's veracity.

Meanwhile, Diana would find Cory Bober's constant badgering to be annoying. It got so bad she filed a restraining order against him.

"My daughter has been missing for six weeks from the Puyallup Fair," Diana wrote in the restraining order. "Cory Bober has called me on a daily basis, telling me my daughter is dead. I was advised by Deputy Brian Coburn to file this complaint if I felt threatened."

The order would only last two weeks. Diana would then call the courts and rescind her request. She would later call Bober and apologize. Her daughter had been missing for over 56 days. Bober was annoying as hell but he was the only one doing research. The only one who cared.

Bober organized a volunteer search for Misty in the Green River area. He somehow coerced someone on the police forensic team to tell him the general vicinity of where one of the Puyallup girl's body was found. Bober surmised that Misty's body would be found in the same general area.

Seventy-two days after Misty had gone missing, there was now a volunteer team searching for her.

Nothing came out of the search.

But Diana would later spot Rheuban at a grocery store and confront him. The young man ran and got into a truck with an older man. She saw the look of fear and apprehension on both men as they sped off.

Diana would then lapse into a depression. She tried to commit suicide with booze and prescription drugs.

The next day she would wake up in a hospital. She would spend the next day there, drying out until being discharged back into the nightmare that had become her life.

A PLEA TO THE PUBLIC

Four months after Misty's disappearance, Diana would appear on a local TV station for a special on the Green River Killer. Jim Doyon, the homicide detective who worked the case, spoke of the killings but deferred on stating if Delange and Chebetnoy(the slain Puyallup girls) were connected.

Doyon took an interest in Misty's case. He would journey to Highway 410 and search near milepost 30 where the bodies of Delange and Chebetnoy had been discovered.

Like Bober and the volunteer search team, he too came up empty.

Bober was undaunted and organized another search. He realized that they had been searching in the wrong spot. They were searching on the south side of the highway when the should have been searching on the north.

Twelve people would show up for the search. Diana would arrive with her older sister, Debra. Bober would arrive with Al Hensley, the father of one of the slain Puyallup girls along with his 14-year old Boy Scout nephew, Jaremy Brown.

It would be the Boy Scout that would make the find

Poking into a ditch with his stick, he saw the crumpled blue jeans. Socks fell out of the jeans.

Baggy and stone-washed, they were cuffed at the bottom. The same jeans that Misty had borrowed from her mother on the night of the fair. The jeans were too big for her and Diana remembered them cuffing them on the bottom.

Bober became excited. He knew that the killer had planted the jeans there as a taunt.

He was right. The police were wrong.

But Diana, according to her sister, "broke into a million pieces."

THE KILLING FIELD

Seven dead women had been found in the nine-mile stretch between Enumclaw and Greenwater in the eight years prior to Misty's disappearance.

The two slain Puyallup girls were found in the same area in 1988 and 1991, only one hundred feet apart. They were left off a footpath that had been hidden by thick brush.

Both of the teenage girls had been presumed abducted from the Puyallup shopping center. Detective Jim Doyon believed privately that the cases were connected. He arrived at the site where Misty's jeans were found and interviewed witnesses, particularly Diana and Bober.

The jeans were taken to the lab and the forensic analysis indicated that the jeans had been in the ditch for some time.

Police suspected that someone (Bober? Diana?) had planted the jeans there.

What was undeniable that the jeans were found only a ten minute walk away from where the bodies of the two slain Puyallup girls were found.

SUSPICIONS ARISE

People began to talk. There were reporters who believed the jeans were planted there. Some were talking as if Diana and Bober were lovers and had plotted this for some insurance money.

Dede Miles, a fifteen-year-old friend of Misty, would come to Sgt. Carver with a tip. She said there was a boy that kept coming over to Misty's parties. He would always leave before her mother came home.

His name was Rheuban Schmidt.

Finally, the unkempt looking young man would come under the radar of the police.

Diana, meanwhile, began to suspect Cory Bober.

How did he know where to look? Why was this stranger so interested in the case to begin with? How did he know so much?

The police had warned her to stay away from him. Now she felt compelled to tell the police of her suspicions.

"Diana comes to station. Now feels Cory Bober may be involved in Misty's disappearance. I asked Diana to submit a written statement to that effect and why she feels he may be involved – she agreed to do so."

Carver's notes

AN INTERVIEW WITH TRINA

Detective Jim Doyon would interview the fifteen-year-old Trina Bevard, the last person to see Misty alive.

Six months had passed. Doyon had brought along the jeans with him, the sight of which made Trina cry.

"It seems to me like something that Misty was wearing that night," Trina said. "It looks very close to what Misty was wearing. The socks, they match what she was wearing. The jeans are big, so – her jeans were baggy that night, that she was wearing. They're – they were light blue like they are in the photo. It just seems, you know, it was the clothes that she was wearing."

Doyon would go on to ask what she was wearing (a pullover) and if she had any jewelry. He then asked if she had any cigarettes or birth control pills.

"No," Trina said. "She was straight. She was a virgin. She didn't smoke, she didn't drink, she didn't do drugs. She was clean, so she had no reason to do anything. She wasn't sexually active."

Trina then revealed that the girls made five calls to Rheuban. They could not get a hold of him. They finally got him on the line and he still refused to pick them up even when the girls offered him money. Misty told him about a key under the front doormat of her home. He could go inside, get money for gas and come pick them up.

Trina stated that she didn't trust Rheuban but only because he didn't keep his word and come pick them up. She then called a 23-year old friend named Mike Rhyner for a ride but they got disconnected. The girls were then stranded. They walked downtown to get to the bus stop before spotting a phone booth by a convenience store. Misty then called her mother, telling her that if Rheuban didn't come pick her up she would take the bus. The two argued as Diana didn't want Misty around Rheuban.

Trina had to get home by 10 p.m. She had about an hour and a half to get home which wasn't that far. Misty could not walk the ten miles to Spanaway.

Trina then decided to walk. She gave Misty her extra money for the bus.

"At that time I made my decision of walking home and she said she would take the bus," Trina recalled. "The last words that I said to her were 'Be careful,' and she turned around and told me the same and we walked off in different directions"

Trina also dismissed the notion of Misty being a runaway.

" Her mom just bought her a stereo and she was so excited and she went shopping and she got new clothes,"Trina recalled. She was telling me all about it. She was really excited about it.

BOBER GOES TO JAIL

Meanwhile, Bober would be sentenced to fourteen months in prison for the marijuana possession. He felt that the sentencing was too punitive and threatened law enforcement that they would never find Misty without him. His fellow inmates thought he was crazy and began calling him "snitch" and "The Green River Killer".

Jail would not slow down Bober's efforts, however. He continued to research and write Misty's mother.

"Dear Diana,

...When we found Misty's clothes, part of me died and I watched a part of you die too (much more than a "part") and I was at a total loss for words. I never wanted to be the one to show you your most horrible fears were true and that your daughter is truly dead at the hands of a sick murderer. I will never rest until the killer (Randy Achziger) is brought to justice and dead, if it takes my life to do it."

AMERICA'S MOST WANTED

Misty's case would eventually be broadcast nationally as it was featured on the America's Most Wanted television show.

Over twenty-eight tips came into Sgt. Carver from people who watched the broadcast.

When the tips went nowhere, Diana's suspicions returned to her original suspect, Rheuban Schmidt. She wanted Carver to speak to the young man but the Sergeant would take a circuitous route to get to Schmidt.

Carver would speak to Frank Rodriguez, the owner of Adam's Ribs, a restaurant where Rheuban worked. He convinced the owner to try and find out how much Rheuban knew about Misty.

"3-4-93 @ 1500: Frank states Rheuban said the following during a lengthy conversation about Misty Copsey:

- Yeah, I know about it.

- I know exactly where she is buried.

- They found the clothes but she is buried 6 miles from there.

- They're off by 6 or 6 1/2 miles."

— Excerpt from Carver's notes

Carver would then wait for Rheuban outside the restaurant before his shift started. Schmidt arrived, saw the cops and immediately ran off. The detectives would eventually catch up with him.

Rheuban would concede that he had received calls from Misty the night of her disappearance. But his story corroborated with Trina's, he told the girls he had no gas and could not pick them up.

Carver then asked if he knew where Misty was buried but Rheuban was adamant that he "said those things to get Frank off my back."

Rheuban then revealed that he suffered from "black outs". He stated that he did not recall anything until the daylight hours of September 18th, 1992.

The detectives pounced, asking if it was possible that he blacked out, picked up Misty and harmed her.

Rheuban claimed he didn't know.

All he knew was that he drove out to his grandmother's farmhouse and couldn't recall why.

Detectives would then give Rheuban a polygraph test.

They would later state that the suspect "zoned out" during the test, nearly falling asleep. The tests were inconclusive but detectives felt as if he were trying to beat the test.

A LITTLE LIE

Rheuban fell off the detective's radar when Carver talked to Dede Miles again. Dede would tell the detective that Trina had not walked home from the fairground like she told him.

Dede said that Trina had a boyfriend come pick her up and didn't want anyone to know.

Trina's boyfriend's name was Michael J. Rhyner. He had nothing on his record aside from traffic stops but he had friends that were connected with Chebetnoy and Delange.

He also had a complaint when he was sixteen years old. He was accused of an abduction rape wherein he used a knife and a cigarette lighter to terrorize an eleven-year-old.

Charges were never filed for an undisclosed reason.

Carver brought Trina in for more questioning. He wanted the truth. The truth about who picked her up that night. The truth about Misty.

But the truth was that Trina told the Sgt. Carver and Detective Tom Matison that she lied because she feared "getting into trouble with her guardian about it."

Trina admitted that she called Rhyner, got disconnected and left a message. She told Misty that they could both ride with Rhyner but Misty said no.

"Trina would not be specific why Misty did not trust Rhyner, but the indication was that Rhyner might have 'come on' to Misty at one time and she did not like it. Trina states that she and Rhyner are friends, but not involved."

— Matison's notes

Trina said that she started to walk and then Rhyner picked her up and dropped her off. The detectives asked if perhaps Rhyner had picked up Misty but she said no.

FRANK RODRIGUEZ' FOLLOW UP

Diana would state that Frank Rodriguez, Rheuban's employer, would call her to say that Rheuban had "bragged about doing something" to Misty with his uncle. Frank didn't fully believe him, however, as Rheuban was "weird" and always bragging about stuff he didn't do.

Diana then approached Carver about Rheuban and the sergeant went ballistic.

"We have our man!" he said.

The man he sought was Michael Rhyner, Trina Bevard's boyfriend.

"We share our knowledge of Mike Rhyner and how he is involved with Misty and Trina – and the fact Trina lied to Doyon. We state that there is an excellent possibility that Rhyner may be linked to Chebetnoy and DeLange. Exchange of information is extremely beneficial."

— Carver's notes

"Sgt. Carver believes that Rhyner dropped Bevard off, returned to the area of the fairgrounds, located Misty Copsey, convinced her to get into his vehicle and drove off with her."

— Doyon's notes

Police set up a sting on Rhyner. The car mechanic was selling his 1981 blue Ford Escort for $200 bucks.

The buyer was an undercover cop.

He watched as Rhyner hurriedly took out trash from the car before the sale. The police then did a forensic examination of the car.

Meanwhile, Rheuban's green Nova was being crushed at a wrecking yard. The Puyallup police didn't care as the tweaker was no longer on their radar. Also, Randy Achziger, Bober's suspect, had been charged and convicted for the rape of a seven-year-old.

INTERROGATING RHYNER

Ideally, Detectives Matison and Sgt. Carver wanted the forensics back from Rhyner's Escort before they spoke to him. But the wait became interminable and they brought him in for questioning without some evidence to back up their suspicions.

Rhyner's story would match that of Trina's. He picked Trina up and went back home. He said that he and Trina were only "good friends" and he had met Misty only four times. Matison then asked Rhyner if he felt Misty was alive and what should happen to the person who harmed her.

Rhyner knew what the detective was getting at. On his own volition, Rhyner told the detectives about his juvenile complaint from years ago. He stated he had been cleared and knew that was why they were looking at him now.

"First thing I thought, you know, well, that's in my file," Rhyner said. "Now you guys are going to think I did it since it's in my file. About Misty, that's the one thing that worried me."

Rhyner then passed a polygraph test.

Grasping at straws, the police then turned their sights back on Rheuban. If only they had impounded his car when they had the chance...

TOO LITTLE TOO LATE

"Rheuban Schmidt's initial interview with Sgt. Carver and I created more questions than answers. He was very vague about what he did that September 17th and finally said that he had a 'blackout' and 'woke up' at his grandmother's property near Enumclaw.

...Schmidt had told Frank Rodriguez that Misty's body was six miles from where the jeans were found. He now claims that he said this just to get Rodriguez "off his back," and was not a true statement.

He was driving a Green Chev Nova at the time but he no longer has the vehicle. It was repossessed.

Schmidt also mentioned that his Grandmother's property is located in King County by Buckley and is over a hundred acres. The property has cows on it. Few people enter onto the property."

— Matison's notes

Tinsley, fifteen years old at the time of Misty's disappearance, told police the Rheuban was his roommate for only a few months. He described Rheuban as a short-tempered guy who had a thirteen-year-old girlfriend. The girlfriend, Tinsley said, got jealous when Rheuban got a call from Misty.

Tinsley stated that Rheuban had left the apartment in a huff then came back between eleven and one at night.

So Rheuban did not "black out" as he told detectives. N

"What do you think might have happened to her?" Matison asked.

"Um, I couldn't, I couldn't say because I have no idea," Tinsley said.

"Well, can you speculate?"

"With Rheuban, this is just that I, this, this is what I say with Rheuban because I, I figure that um that he, he tried to, he tried to um, get with her or something and she said, she said no and he got all pissed and did something, I don't know, that's just a second guess."

"You think Rheuban would be capable of ah, kidnapping and killing somebody?"

"I think he could," Tinsley said.

Detectives would meet with Rheuban again, relaying the information that Tinsley recalled him coming back to the apartment that night.

But Rheuban remained adamant in stating that he didn't remember what he did. The detectives then drove him out to his grandmother's farm which had over 100-acres...100 secluded acres.

Detective Matison would note that Rheuban's grandmother's house six miles north of Buckley. Rheuban told Frank that Misty would be buried six miles away from where her jeans were found which would place it in the close vicinity of his grandmother's farm. They would go to inquire with his grandmother but she was not home.

They did not follow-up with the grandmother .

Even so, Rheuban's story no longer held up. He told Misty that he didn't have any gas. He lived sixteen miles away from the fair.

But then he stated that he had driven to his grandmother's farm in Buckley then returned home.

A sixty-mile round trip.

Detectives would give him another polygraph test which he passed.

"It appears that Rheuban Schmidt was not involved in the disappearance of Misty Copsey. He, however, has no alibi as to his movements during the evening of her disappearance, as well as no memory; he claimed that he had a blackout. He acknowledges that he left the residence of James Tinsley, but does not remember what he did.

Investigation to continue."

— Matison's notes

ONE YEAR ANNIVERSARY

The local media ran a few more stories on Misty's disappearance as the Puyallup Fair started. The forensic test on Rhyner's test finally came through. There was no match

with Misty anywhere.

Now once again grasping at straws, Carver would turn to Diana and her associates. He would interview Diana's parole officer and one of her ex-boyfriends.

Misty's father, Buck, was asked to take a polygraph test. He gave consent and passed.

"I explained to her that missing person investigations, at some point in time, must eliminate the parents of any wrongdoing. Diana agreed to the examination."

— Carver's notes

Diana would pass her polygraph test but Jim Corey, Doyon's colleague, said that Diana's polygraph would prove to be inconclusive and that perhaps she had something to do with planting the jeans at the location on Hwy 410.

Carver had always had his doubts about Diana and felt that she planted the jeans.

But the leads would eventually dry up. After nine years, Misty Copsey's disappearance would turn cold.

No one was ever charged with her disappearance.

THE AFTERMATH

Diana would hand out fliers at the Puyallup Fairgrounds every year. She was doing more than law enforcement and even the media.

Every now and then, a local reporter would run a story about Misty. A few cranks would call in and say that they knew something but it would lead to nowhere. Then that would be it. Everything would run dry.

Detective Jim Doyon felt that she was deceased.

BOBER TO THE RESCUE

Bober was then caught for marijuana possession again but this time, he pressed for an advantage. He would gain the Washington State Patrol crime lab report on Misty's jeans, compiled after their 1993 discovery.

He argued that the lab report was part of his defense....he gambled and won.

Obtaining the prized document, the amateur sleuth went to work. The report stated there was no blood, no semen. But there were hairs, fibers, and three red paint chips. There were also holes in the left leg in the jeans, above the knee.

Bober knew that somehow, someway, Randy Achziger was involved. That he killed Misty.

The forensic details raced through Bober's head...red paint chips...red paint chips...

He knew that Bober had a red Porsche. He knew that the paint chips would match.

But the police had another suspect they didn't tell anyone about.

Robert Leslie Hickey.

Hickey's hunting ground was the Puyallup area where he specialized in abduction rapes.

He also drove a red Camaro.

Puyallup police had him on their list as a possible suspect but he was never questioned nor did they obtain forensic samples from his car.

Thirteen years later, however, they would collect samples from Achziger's old car. The car had been sold and the new owner was open to having forensics performed on it.

The particles would be sent to a crime lab which already had a backlog of over a year.

With nothing else left to do, the police turned once again to Rheuban Schmidt.

"I think it's worth taking another shot at Schmidt, and we're planning on it. He's been clean since 1993 ...

— Excerpt from notes by Lt. Dave McDonald, March 19, 2006

Only Schmidt had not been clean. He had been convicted of second-degree theft in 2000. In early 1996, he was accused of rape by one of Misty's best friends. He had held a pillow over her face to silence her but two weeks after filing the report, the girl back away from her accusation and did not file charges.

"[She] told me that she would be undergoing counseling related to the rape, but that she did not want to undergo any additional stress that may be caused by further investigation or possible prosecution in this matter.

Case cleared exceptional/refused by victim."

— Pierce County sheriff's report, Feb. 6, 1996

Later in 2006, Puyallup police gathered more reports on Rheuban. One was a domestic violence protection order requested by his wife, the mother of his three children.

"Rheuban has previously told her that if she ever had him served with a court order he'd 1) burn her house down with her and her kids in it, and 2) send 'some guys' to kick in her door and take money from her.

(She) said Rheuban told her that they'd get money from her if they had to beat her, rape her and then rob her.

(She) said Rheuban told her that if it came to that she 'wouldn't be breathing' when they were done with her."

— Pierce County Sheriff's report, Nov. 9, 2006

MISSING PAINT CHIPS

Adding more incompetence to the investigation, the red paint chips found on Misty's jeans would turn up "missing." All that remained inside the bag where the chips were marked was a piece of plastic.

The lab technicians now had no way to match the red chips on Misty's jeans to Achziger's red Porsche.

Bober would claim that the red chips did match and the police were now trying to save face. Diana, however, no longer wants anything to do with him.

Bober would state that the police would tell Diana that they had, in fact, tested the red paint found on Misty's clothes against Achziger's Porsche. Bober discovered that the red paint was missing beforehand yet the police would lie to Diana about the test.

The lies and incompetence that began investigation have seemingly ended it as well. The Puyallup police relied far too heavily on polygraph tests to discount suspects where their own accounts (particularly in the case of Schmidt) were shaky at best. They failed to secure possession of Schmidt's Green Nova which may have proven to provide forensic evidence that Misty was in his vehicle.

Twenty-four years have elapsed since Misty's disappearance.

Her case remains unsolved.

MISSING TIFFANY

ANA BENTON

The Disappearance of Tiffany Daniels

As shocking as it might seem, there are over 100,000 missing person cases active in the United States this very second. While the majority of them are eventually found, there is a large percentage of those who have been gone for years. The police extended their investigations as much as they could, and they reached the very end because there was no new information. Finally, those cases simply turn cold.

Missing person cases are particularly difficult for both families and friends. All of them are left without answers about what happened to their loved one, and they are constantly waiting for a break in the case, hoping they will have closure. The Daniels family lived through all of this in the summer of 2013 when their daughter Tiffany went missing one afternoon. It is one of the most perplexing cases in the history of Pensacola, Florida that still puzzles the investigators.

Early life

Tiffany Daniels was born on March 11th, 1988 in Dallas, Texas. She grew up in a loving and supportive family who encouraged her to follow her dreams from an early age. Tiffany loved arts, and that was evident since her high school days. She was very creative and would spend days working on a single painting. Tiffany was not shy at all and had many friends who loved spending time with her because she was always happy and positive.

After finishing high school, Tiffany felt the need to change her scenery so she moved out to Pensacola, Florida. The city had everything Tiffany craved for – long beaches, beautiful nature, and great artistic community. She was an avid hiker and loved spending time in nature. Not to forget that she often went camping on her own just to clear up her mind and relax. Tiffany loved animals, and she was a pescetarian, meaning that her diet didn't contain any meat except for the fish. She also accepted a position at Pensacola State College theater as a set designer. The pay was not spectacular, but Tiffany was doing what she loved, and she could release her artistic side.

Tiffany liked to express herself through dancing as well. It was the perfect way for her to wind down, and she would frequent blues and swing parties downtown. Everyone in those circles knew Tiffany and loved her house gatherings too. Once the dance party comes to an end, Tiffany's friends would get in their vehicles and continue having fun at her home. She was spontaneous, loved the people around her, and enjoyed life to the fullest.

Unfortunately, her caring nature got her into financial problems. Tiffany mostly lived with roommates because she was not able to cover the whole rent herself. However, those roommates would often miss their payments, and Tiffany felt bad for them. She would always pay their share even though she was struggling herself. Unfortunately, those roommates would use her kindness, and they never pay Tiffany back. In the end, Tiffany's bank account was almost empty, and she was looking for a responsible roommate who could actually afford to live with her. She ended up placing a Craigslist ad, hoping she would have more luck with the next roommate.

Gary Nichols who was 54 years old at the time saw the ad and contacted Tiffany since he needed a place to stay as soon as possible. Gary was the father of one of Tiffany's friends, and he was going through a divorce. Even though the difference in age was evident, Tiffany accepted her new roommate with open arms, and the two of them started getting along really well. Gary was financially stable, so Tiffany knew that the rent will not be a problem for him. Additionally, they had similar interests because Gary was very active, and both of them followed the same diet. Gary moved in during July of 2013, and Tiffany hoped that her issues with tenants were over.

Tiffany was in a relationship at the time, and her boyfriend's name was Grey Thomas. They met in the summer of 2012 at a dance party and were inseparable since then. He just got accepted to the graduate program at the University of Texas located in Austin. He decided to move there and urged Tiffany to join him. However, Tiffany was not eager to leave Florida, but she still wanted to have a long-distance relationship with him. The two have made plans for her to visit in a couple of weeks, and Tiffany was happy because it was clear he cared about her as well. Grey hoped Tiffany will like Austin and that she would eventually change her mind about moving there.

The day of the disappearance

Tiffany's boyfriend was supposed to head out to Texas on August 11th, 2013 and the two of them met for a breakfast where they said goodbyes to each other. They will be apart for a couple of weeks and simply had to spend some time together before his trip. Gary Nichols saw Tiffany that afternoon, and he did notice that she was a bit sad about the fact that her boyfriend was leaving which was understandable. But she soon started talking about the trip to Austin she was planning and her mood brightened up immediately.

Since Pensacola State College theater was preparing to start the production of the musical called *Spamalot*, Tiffany had a lot of work ahead of her. *Spamalot* was based on the movie called *Monty Python and the Holy Grail* so Tiffany decided to re-watch it just to get inspired. After all, she was in charge of the set and wanted to do a great job. Gary Nichols was at the house, so he joined her in front of the TV set. The two watched the movie up until midnight and then went to sleep. Both of them had to get up early for work. Sometime around 05:00 AM Gary heard the front door opening and closing several times. He thought it must be Tiffany, but he was a bit confused because he knew that she was not an early riser. As a matter of fact, her job started at 08:00 AM so this was very unusual.

Gary got up and went work at 07:00 AM. The first thing he noticed when he exited the house was that Tiffany's car was gone. He assumed she went to work earlier because it was the first day of *Spamalot* production. Tiffany probably wanted to get more things done. Tiffany's boss did confirm that she showed up for work on schedule but asked him to leave earlier. Tiffany also mentioned that she will not be in town for a couple of days and wanted to inform him about it. Tiffany didn't mention where she was going and didn't provide any additional information. The boss simply concluded that she might have some family business, or wanted to go camping. Tiffany left the theater around 04:45 PM.

Gary came home from work as usual but Tiffany wasn't there. It was strange because she didn't mention she was leaving or anything similar. Tiffany was very responsible and would always tell her friends and family about her plans. Even though Gary was her roommate for a short time, he got to know Tiffany and was sure that she would bring up an upcoming trip. Gary called his daughter Noel who was Tiffany's friend and asked her if she knew anything about Tiffany's whereabouts. She told him not to worry and that Tiffany would show up soon because she was probably staying with friends or working overtime.

The power was cut off the next day, and Gary assumed that Tiffany forgot to pay the bills. He tried contacting her, but nobody answered the cell phone. Worried that something happened to her, he once again urged his daughter Noel to contact Tiffany's mother Cindy and see if she could get a hold of her. Noel sent her a Facebook message, and Tiffany's mother brushed it off because her daughter was a free spirit and had a tendency to go out in nature. Perhaps she had no signal, or she didn't hear the phone ringing. But as the days went on without a single word from Tiffany, everyone started feeling a bit uneasy about the situation.

The search for Tiffany

Tiffany's family got really concerned after they realized that they couldn't reach her for several days. Her cell phone kept ringing, but nobody was answering. Cindy Daniels decided to start calling Tiffany's friends to see if anyone knew where her daughter was. She contacted Noel Nichols, and the two of them made a list of people they should contact. As they went through the list, they realized that no one had seen Tiffany for a week and they all assumed she was staying with another friend. Cindy was really worried, and she contacted the law enforcement to report that her daughter was missing.

Cindy went straight to Escambia County sheriff's office, but the law enforcement didn't take her seriously. They did send out a patrol car to her house to take a statement. The officers thought that since Tiffany was young and free-spirited, she is probably somewhere having a blast and she would turn up soon. But Cindy persisted, and they took a closer look at the case. Escambia County sheriff's office realized that the missing person case was not in their jurisdiction because Tiffany lived in Pensacola and that was also the location she was last seen at. Pensacola Police Department was not dismissive of the report, and they were quickly out on the scene.

Cindy was already at Tiffany's place of residence when the detective Daniel Harnett arrived there to investigate if there was anything suspicious in the house. Tiffany's mother was asked to wait in front of the house. The detective and an officer went through the rooms together and found Tiffany's camping gear. This meant that she wasn't taking a break somewhere in the woods. There were also no signs that she packed her things for any type of trip. Detective Harnett asked Cindy about Tiffany's personal life, focusing on her boyfriend Grey Thomas. Cindy told him that he left for Texas one day before Tiffany's disappearance and this made Detective Harnett focus on the possibility that Tiffany decided to follow him there. However, one of Tiffany's closest friends said: *"Tiffany was a very spontaneous person, but she was also a reliable person. My opinion is if she said that she would be somewhere, she would be there."*

Rodney Daniels, Tiffany's father called Grey Thomas to see if she was there with him. He told him that he spoke to Tiffany on the day of his arrival to Texas, but he hasn't heard from her afterward. Knowing that the majority of disappearances are often followed by a murder, Detective Harnett couldn't rule out the option that Grey returned to Pensacola one day later and hurt Tiffany for some reason. He contacted Grey, asking him to go to his local police station and give them his DNA. They needed to have it in a database in case some new evidence turns up during the investigation. Curious about Grey's whereabouts on the day of the disappearance, Detective Harnett requested Grey's cellphone data. It showed that Grey was in Austin, Texas since the day he left Pensacola.

Running out of reasons for the disappearance, the investigators started interviewing the entire family. They started viewing the case as a possible suicide, so Detective Harnett asked a lot of questions about Tiffany's mental state. Her sister Candace McAdams who lived out of state was very close to Tiffany. The two of them spoke over the phone at least a couple of times every week. Candace mentioned that she noticed a change in Tiffany's behavior sometime in 2012. She was not as happy as she used to be and Candace though that she might be keeping something from her. But nobody could be certain that she was depressed or had any mental problems.

After questioning the neighbors, the investigators found out that Tiffany did come back home after work on the day of her disappearance. Her car was seen briefly in front of the house. Gary Nichols was there at the time, but he didn't see her come in. He was talking with his girlfriend on the phone, and the chances are he was simply too engaged in the conversation to register that someone opened the front door. Cindy thought this was strange because the house itself wasn't large. She stated: *"In Tiffany's room the top of her closet had a foot missing of it. Clear through to the next room. You could throw something through it. I find it hard to believe he couldn't hear her through the room but he heard her going in and out of the house early in the morning."* However, the police dismissed Gary as a suspect because there were no traces of foul play anywhere, and he was the first one to start worrying about Tiffany. Detective Hartnett said: *"Gary seemed appropriate. There was nothing unclear in anything he told us to raise an alarm."*

The discovery of the car

Detective Harnett alerted the media right away about Tiffany's 1999 Toyota 4Runner car, hoping that someone might have seen it somewhere. The TV stations broadcasted the images for days, while Tiffany's friends went around Pensacola, putting up the fliers. And soon enough, the police had their first solid lead. Tiffany's car was spotted at a parking lot at Park West in Pensacola Beach. A jogger who was out running on the morning of August 20th, 2013 thought that the vehicle looked familiar and connected the dots. He also knew the Daniels family, as well as Tiffany herself. Tiffany's mother said: *"I felt something bad happened as soon as they located the car. I believed she was still on the island and that we would find her."*

Once the police arrived, they inspected the abandoned car. It was not too dirty from the outside, and it looked like it was out in the elements for a couple of days. They found Tiffany's bicycle on the inside, alongside her purse, a wallet, a cell phone, a couple of paintings, a jar of peanut butter, and a bottle of water. The forensic team analyzed the car and found two suspicious fingerprints on the car and the steering wheel. After a thorough examination, they determined that the fingerprints didn't belong to Tiffany or any of the officers who were on the scene. Then they proceeded to run them through the database but got no hits.

The parking lot where the car was found was right next to the beach. It was a very popular spot for both locals and tourists. Tiffany's friends and family though that someone must have seen something in the days following the disappearance. The police weren't enthusiastic about it because Tiffany's car was not very distinctive and they were certain nobody would have noticed when it arrived or who was driving it. Not to forget that there were two condominium complexes on the other side of the parking lot. It was summertime and people would usually hang out on their balconies, trying to cool down from the heat.

Tiffany's friends started going around, handing out the flyers, and talking to the people living in the apartment buildings. One resident told them that he was sure the car was not in the parking lot two days ago because he has a good view of it and would have noted if a particular vehicle was parked there for a longer period of time. A couple of people said that they saw a man driving and exiting the car. All of the information was written down and presented to the detectives. They were conducting their own investigation at the time that included toll booths at the Bob Sikes Bridge.

Since Park West was located on Santa Rosa Island, only one bridge connected it to the mainland. The bridge has toll booths, and every vehicle that crosses over is captured by the surveillance cameras. Unfortunately, the cameras monitor the license plates only so finding out who was driving the car was impossible. On the other hand, this information would provide the investigators with the exact time when Tiffany's Toyota crossed the bridge. The detectives went through the images of vehicles that entered Santa Rosa Island on the day Tiffany disappeared and discovered that her car passed the toll booths on August 12th, 2013 at 07:51 PM. This was three hours after she left the theater.

The search of Santa Rosa Island

The detectives, as well as the family, had many theories about what might have happened to Tiffany on Santa Rosa Island. The forensic team determined that the tires of her bike had sand on them which led them to speculate that she went on a ride that night. She might have placed the bike in her car and proceeded to the beach to watch the meteor shower or take a swim in the ocean. The currents are incredibly strong in that area, and she could have been pulled under, unable to swim back to the shore.

Led by this thought, the detectives suspected that her body might appear on the shore of Santa Rosa Island. The island itself was large and searching it would be quite a task. Tiffany's parents found out about KLAAS organization that would gather up the volunteers from the area in order to search for missing children. They contacted the people in charge, and they agreed to help out with the search of Santa Rosa Island. The teams had a lot of grounds to cover, but they had plenty of help from the other search organizations in Florida. They searched the island by foot, going through the entire national park. There was no sign of Tiffany or any items that could be connected to her.

The fact that they didn't find any traces was encouraging to Tiffany's family because this meant that she might be alive somewhere. But it was unlikely that she was still on the island. They needed to widen up the search and let everyone know that Tiffany was missing. Noel Nichols decided to set up a Facebook page in order to help find Tiffany. She uploaded her photos as well as the images of her distinctive foot tattoos. Other users were sharing the information, and soon the tips started coming in.

The sightings

Noel sent every single information she got through the Facebook page to the detective working on this case. Detective Daniel Harnett, eager to find Tiffany, was willing to check every possible sighting. A few weeks after setting up the page, Noel received a tip from a local store. A clerk claimed that Tiffany entered the shop and bought some groceries. He was able to provide a full description of the girl which sparked the interest. Unfortunately, Detective Harnett asked for the surveillance tapes, and Tiffany was not on them. The clerk simply wanted to become a part of the investigation at any cost.

But the next possible sighting gave Tiffany's parents hope that she was out there somewhere. A waitress from Metairie, Louisiana sent a message through Facebook in January of 2014 saying that she might have seen Tiffany a couple of weeks after her disappearance. The woman didn't contact anyone because she was not sure if the girl in the restaurant was indeed Tiffany. However, she couldn't stop thinking about it and decided to let the family know. There was something strange about that encounter, and the waitress thought that it might be important.

She recalls that three women came into the restaurant one night. Two of them were younger, while the third one was significantly older than them. The older woman wore expensive clothes, while the other two did not. They also had long sleeved shirts, which was an odd sight in New Orleans during the summer and autumn. The waitress found it unusual that the older woman was the only one communicating with her. The young women simply sat there in silence, trying not to make an eye contact with the waitress. One of them spoke up to ask if the soups on the menu had fish in them, and the waitress took a good look at her face. It seemed familiar to her and she asked right away if she was the woman who went missing in Florida.

The mood at the table shifted instantly. The whole group got up and left the restaurant. The tip sounded credible because Tiffany was a pescetarian, and she was very concerned about her diet. The family asked if the waitress could provide any surveillance videos that would give them proof that Tiffany was there. She told them that the tapes were long gone because they record over the old footage regularly. While this didn't give the investigators any concrete proof that Tiffany was out there, the tip led Tiffany's family to form another theory – that she was a victim of human trafficking.

White Tiffany didn't fit the profile of a typical human trafficking victim, nothing can be dismissed in this case. There was a possibility that she was kidnapped from the beach and transported to New Orleans soon after her disappearance. Tiffany's family dug deeper and found connections with another incident when a young woman was taken to the same city by two men. She was then forced to become a sex worker. Human trafficking is an ongoing problem in the United States, and the police are doing everything in order to prevent it.

However, they simply cannot save all of the victims right away. Instead, they are familiar with the known human trafficking routes and the local patrol cars often monitor the movement on them. One of the routes is the Interstate 10 that passes through Pensacola. This very fact made Tiffany's parents believe that she met someone on the night of the disappearance and they probably took advantage of her. Tiffany was friendly and loved talking to other people. She might have bumped into someone who seemed trusting but had bad intentions. Unfortunately, the police still had little information, and they were unable to pursue this tip. The case remained open, but there were no new leads.

The revival of the case

The Investigation Discovery channel was aware of the case, and they decided to include it in the new season of their popular show called *Disappeared.* In it, they cover the missing person cases hoping that the media exposure would prompt the possible witnesses to contact the authorities and provide them with new details that could revive the case. Their crew visited Pensacola and talked to almost everyone involved with the investigation, including the lead detective and

Tiffany's parents. The whole city knew that the Investigation Discovery crew was there and people were once again talking about the case.

Four months after they completed the filming, Pensacola Police Department was contacted by a new eyewitness who claimed they had information about the case. The witness told Detective Hartnett that they saw a man opening the trunk of Tiffany's car on the parking lot in Park West. The man was wearing red shorts, and he was in his thirties. This confirmed the statements made by the tenants from the nearby apartment building who claimed that the vehicle was driven by a man. Unfortunately, they weren't able to identify the said individual.

Tiffany Daniels' disappearance is still being investigated, and the authorities are hoping that someone will come forward soon. There has not been a confirmed sighting since August 12th, 2013 but they are not ruling out the possibility that she is alive. The investigators never found her body, so any scenario is possible. The family and friends are managing the Facebook page about Tiffany, and they are updating it regularly, doing their best to keep her in the media. The case remains a true mystery that will hopefully be resolved one day.

THE MISSING IRISH WOMEN

ANDREA TORRENCE

Ireland's Vanishing Triangle

Between March 1993 and July 1998, eight young women vanished from the face of the Earth. The disappearance of the women has been dubbed "Ireland's Vanishing Triangle" by the media. The women were all last seen in the Leinster Province in eastern Ireland and none of their bodies have ever been recovered. To date, the mysterious Vanishing Triangle still troubles the families of the young women, police investigators, conspiracy theorists, and all of the peoples of Ireland.

The people missing women in the Ireland's Vanishing Triangle case all had very specific similarities: they were young, ranging from their teenagers to around 40 years old; their disappearances were sudden and without any significant clues for police to track despite the several large scale searches by Irish police force (Gardaí Síochána); and they all went missing after in the same geographical location.

The name "Vanishing Triangle" refers to the triangular shape of the location in the eastern part of the island, all within the boundaries of the Leinster Province. The unofficial list for the missing women in the Vanishing Triangle consists of six women, but a total of eight women have been reported missing within the same time frame and location of the others. Some speculate that, because of the similarities and oddities of the eight women's disappearances, they all became victims to a serial killer who frequented the Leinster Province during that period.

The cases of the Vanishing Triangle are still often featured in Irish media from time to time, even after a two decade-long search for the victims. They have also become the subject in numerous documentaries about unsolved crimes, including the TV-3 production of "Disappeared in the Mountains" by a local Irish TV station. Operation Trace is an effort by the Guardaí to solve this case of eight missing persons but has yet to yield substantial results, despite the promise of a €10,000 reward for information that leads to the recovery of any of the eight women's bodies.

There are a total of eight missing women in the Ireland's Vanishing Triangle case. The terrifying disappearances began in 1993 with Annie McCarrick – a 26-year old from New York who was taking her undergraduate studies in Ireland. She chose to continue go to college in Ireland in order to reconnect with her country's history and family heritage. She lived in an apartment with two female roommates in Sandymount, a suburb located on the Southside of Dublin. In March 1993, Annie was excitedly waiting for her mother, Nancy McCarrick, to visit her in Ireland.

On Friday, March 26th, only a few days before her mother's arrival, Annie was expected to come to her office to collect her paycheck but she never came. Previously, Annie made dinner plans with her friend, Hilary Brady, and his girlfriend, Rita Fortune, at her apartment on Saturday, March 27th. Her friends found it odd that Annie, who had arranged the whole appointment, was not in her apartment and her roommates had no idea where she had gone to. They immediately contacted Annie's parents in New York to inform them of their missing daughter.

Her father, John McCarrick, immediately had the feeling that something was wrong. "She was always reaching out and touching someone," he told reporters in an interview. "She would never have gone a day without talking to someone. We were very, very concerned." Both Nancy and John immediately boarded a plane to Ireland where they could help in the hunt for their missing daughter. The search for Annie became one of Ireland's largest wide scale searches for a missing person in the country's history.

Testimonies from witnesses place Annie in a local bank and grocery store on the morning of her disappearance. Another witness said that Annie was on a No. 44 city bus headed towards the small village of Enniskerry. The night of her disappearance, several pub-goers recalled seeing Annie at Johnny's Pub, located three miles past the borders of Enniskerry and at the foot of the Wicklow Mountains. The terrifying thing about this testimony is that witnesses said that she was accompanied by an unknown man. At the time, nobody was aware of Annie being involved in a relationship with a man so the Gardaí had no leads or suspects. After six months of fruitless searching, Nancy and John returned to the United States.

This was just the beginning of the Vanishing Triangle case of missing women in Leinster Province in Ireland. Just 3 months after Annie's disappearance, the family of Eva Brennan would receive the same heart-shattering news of a missing loved one. Corlette, Eva's sister, told reporters, "I remember seeing [Annie's] father on the television in Ireland and remember seeing the sorrow and the sadness and the anguish on that family's face... I couldn't imagine anybody going through that. But it was a very short 12 weeks later that [our family] were going through the exact same thing with Eva."

Eva Brennan, aged 39 at the time of her disappearance, was a local of Rathgar, Dublin. She went missing on July 25, 1993, only several months after Annie McCarrick. Eva's family recall her being extremely depressed after departing from a family lunch at her parents' home in Rathgar. Her father, Davy, went to her apartments after not receiving any news from his daughter for two days. After ringing her doorbell several times to no avail, he asked the barman at his family-owned pub, the Horse and Hound Pub, to assist him in breaking a window at Eva's apartment in order to enter the premises. Upon entering, Davy remembered seeing the jacket that she had worn to the family lunch.

After reporting their missing daughter to the Gardaí, their case was put on hold for a whole three months before any official investigation was launched. The family has openly criticized the Gardaí for mishandling Eva's disappearance. Similar to the search for Annie McCarrick, the police found no substantial evidence of where Eva would disappear to and why. Rumors circulated and were reported by some members of the Irish Police Force that Eva was an acquaintance of the infamous double-killer Michael Bambrick who was convicted of killing and hiding the bodies of Patricia McGauley and Mary Cummins in Clondalkin, Dublin.

Corlette expressed her doubt that she even knew Bambrick. She further stated that nobody had ever known of Eva stepping foor into Clondalkin, Dublin, or the southern city where Bambrick originated from. Corlette mentioned that Eva would visit her parents' home every day, would have lunch with them, and then retire to her apartment. Eva was not one to go out and socialize with others, let alone get close with a person who was well-known for murdering two women.

A full five months would pass before another woman was added to the growing list of missing people in the Vanishing Triangle case. On January 3, 1994, Imelda Keenan, a 22-year old native from Mountmellick, vanished in the city of Waterford. She was registered as a student taking computer courses at Central Technical Institute at the time of her disappearance. Initially, Imelda went to stay with one of her brothers living in Cobh, County Cork. After a brief visit, she departed for Waterford where she would spend a couple nights with two other brothers. At the time of her disappearance, Imelda was sharing an apartment with her boyfriend, Mark Wall, in on William Street in Waterford.

On the day of her disappearance, Imelda told Mark that she was going to the post office to run some errands. She left their apartment at around 1:30 PM and she walked down William Street onto Lombard Street. Imelda was sighted whilst she was crossing the road by a local doctor's secretary with whom she was well acquainted with. The secretary and a friend saw Imelda crossing the road near the Tower Hotel. That was the last time Imelda was ever seen or heard from again.

A Garda search for Imelda was soon conducted but produced nothing. The search for the Central Technical Institute by her family and friends has been going on for over 20 years, and the €10,000 reward for information leading to the discover of Imelda's whereabouts remains unclaimed. Her mother Elizabeth passed away in 2008 before finding getting closure on her missing daughter's case. "I don't think mammy could rest in peace," Imelda's brother Donal told reporters through tears. "Every mother likes to know where her baby is. That's what we want to know, we need our sister." Donal broke down and got onto his hands and knees during a gravesite ceremony in County Laois, begging for the return of their missing sister.

Donal added, "We are not looking for justice for Imelda. We are looking for Imelda. We do not wish for anyone to be held [accountable] for what may or may not have happened to [her]. We just want Imelda." He let the public know that the family will not charge any suspect for whatever misfortune has happened to his sister. "Closure for you and closure for the Keenan family is what's at stake."

After one year and ten months since Imelda disappeared, Josephine "JoJo" Dollard went missing on November 9, 1995. JoJo, 21-years old at the time, lived with a sister in a small village in County Kilkenny. She was raised by her older sisters who constantly worried for JoJo when she left the quiet town of Kilkenny to pursuit a career as a beautician in Dublin. On the date of her disappearance, she met with some friends in Dublin. She was supposed to take a bus and arrive at Kilkenny that evening, but she the time slipped her mind whilst chatting with friends and she ended up missing the bus for her return trip home. JoJo decided to hitchhike her way back to Kilkenny which was a common mode of transport for women in Ireland during that period.

Geraldine Niland – a journalist who wrote books on cases of missing women in Ireland – wrote the story of JoJo's return trip back to Kilkenny based on the testimonies of people who contacted her moments before her disappearance. After deciding to hitchhike home, Geraldine wrote that "Her first ride took her halfway to the little town of Moone. She phoned a friend from a phone box there, and told [her] that she was hitching a ride and waiting for another ride to come along." As she was talking to her friend, JoJo ended their conversation abruptly. "When [JoJo] was talking with her friend, she said, 'Oh, a car is coming, and I have to go now.' And she put the phone down. And that is the last we heard of Jojo Dollard."

Mary Phelan, one of JoJo's older sister and caregiver, remembered a brief conversation they had before JoJo's decision to move to the big city. "I gave her a little ring and a little bracelet," she says and she reminisces about her baby sister, "and I'll always remember in the room, she says to me, 'Mary, when I finish my beauty course in Dublin, I'll come home to you and I'll do your hair and I'll have you looking nice.' And I never saw her again. It's terrible."

Mary has done everything in her power to put pressure on the authorities to keep JoJo's case alive. She was inspired by the incredible story of a father who was in her exact same position: John McCarrick, father of Annie McCarrick. "I admired her dad," Mary told reporters about her initial response to seeing John on the television. "I thought, 'My God, what is that man going through? What is he really going through? [...] If John can go out there and do so much for Annie, then why can't I do it [for JoJo]? He was a great influence on me."

The next victim of Ireland's Vanishing Triangle was Fiona Pender. Fiona was added to the growing list of missing people in August 24, 1996, after her family reported to the authorities that their daughter's whereabouts were unknown. Fiona, 25-years old at the time and a native from Tullamore, County Offaly, was last seen by her boyfriend, John Thompson, as she was leaving her apartment building. The part-time model was seven months pregnant at the time of her disappearance. She reportedly went shopping for baby clothes the previous day.

The weeks following the initial report of Fiona's disappearance were filled with fruitless searching in local bogs, forests and rivers. Even the four-mile long Royal Canal was drained as investigators became desperate to find Fiona. A year after her disappearance, the police arrested five people and interrogated them about Fiona's whereabouts but were subsequently released without charge.

Not much information is available regarding the days prior to her disappearance. However, unlike the other women mentioned previously in this article, recent findings by the Gardaí have led to believe that Fiona died not long after vanishing. A suspect's wife came forward in 2014 with vital information that led to the arrest of her husband who she thinks murdered Fiona in 1996. The wife was allegedly assaulted by her husband who then told her that he would do "what [he] did to Fiona." The wife is currently in protective custody abroad.

The husband, now in his 40s, was captured abroad and charged with battery. Upon capture, the authorities received information that the body of Fiona could be found buried beneath a piece of farmland nearby Tullamore.

On February 13, 1997, Ciara Breen became the next missing person to be added to the names of missing women in the Ireland's Vanishing Tirangle case. Ciara was 18 years old at the time of her disappearance, and she was last seen by her mother Bernadette who said that they had just retired to their bedrooms after midnight. Bernadette got up at around 2 AM to use the bathroom and discovered that Ciara was not in her room. Her window was left open, and it is believed that Ciara did this intentionally to return back to her room after sneaking out. Authorities believe that she left her room to meet with an unknown person in the middle of the night, but no evidence points in that direction.

Since she disappeared, there have been two credible sightings of Ciara on the night she vanished. In 2015, Liam Mullen was taken into police custody following a lead that he was involved in Ciara's disappearance, but was soon released without being charged. He soon became the chief suspect in Ciara's case and was arrested again in 2017 following a suspicion of drunk driving. Before being under arrest, Mullen swallowed a substance that caused him to become ill. The on-call doctor at the Garda station was summoned to attend to the unconscious man, but despite their efforts to resuscitate the dying man, Mullen silently passed away and was pronounced dead on the spot. There was no proof that states the police had mishandled the man in any way.

Friends of Ciara told the authorities that Mullen had approached them on the day before she went missing. The friends overheard their plans to rendezvous the following night. Mullen denied ever having the conversation with Ciara, and although lands belonging to Mullen and his family were searched, the police did not find any conclusive evidence of his involvement in Ciara's missing persons case until his 2017 arrest.

Fiona Sinnott, 19-years old at the time and a native of Rosslare, County Wexford, was went missing on February 9, 1989. She was currently residing in Broadway during that period. Reports say that on February 8th, Sinnott had just left a pub with Sean Carroll – her ex-boyfriend and father of their 11-month old daughter. While being interrogated by investigators, Carroll said that he escorted Sinnott back to her home in Bayhitt, and added that he spent the night on her couch.

That night, Sinnott had been complaining about arm and upper body pains and decided to go straight to bed. On the morning of her disappearance, Caroll allegedly walked into Sinnott's room and found her wide awake. She told him that she was still experiencing pain and was planning on hitchhiking to the hospital later that day. Carroll reportedly gave her £3 for the trip and left her house. He was picked up by his mother who drove him back to their family home where their 11-month old daughter was staying at the time. This was the last time anyone had seen or heard from Sinnott for the last 20 years.

Investigations by the police found that Sinnott had not met with a doctor that day since there were no medical records of her visit or any scheduled surgeries. The authorities failed to produce evidence that she had even attempted to hitchhike to the hospital. While investigating in her house, the Gardaí found that it had been emptied of many of her personal possessions. Alan Bailey, a retired detective who was tasked with investigating Sinnott's disappearance, told reporters that, "There was a complete absence of clothing and other personal items indicating that a teenage girl and her 11-month old daughter were actually living there."

News of Sinnott's disappearance spread, and a local farmer informed the Gardaí that he discovered several black garbage bags in the corner of his fields. The contents of the bags were documents and items with Sinnott's name written on them. The farmer initially set the bags on fire as he thought they were just evidence of illegal dumping.

It wasn't until February 18th, a full nine days after her disappearing, that she was reported missing to the authorities. Fiona's father, Pat, alerted the police of the situation when he contacted the Kimore Garda Station. He informed them that his daughter had not been sighted since the 8th. The Gardaí responded with a full-scale investigation of a missing persons.

The Gardaí have treated this case as a murder investigation and believe that the suspect behind Sinnott's disappearance is a person who as well acquainted with her. The police searched lakes and body dump sites but have returned empty handed. Within the first few weeks of the investigation, one witness told police that they had heard a woman's scream in the Millpond Cross area on the same night Fiona reportedly left the pub with Carroll. Another witness, a passing motorist, reported seeing a couple on the side of the road who were in a heated argument. Neither reports had been proven nor linked back to Sinnott's case.

Many people believe that Wexford residents are trying their best to cover up what happened to Sinnott. Rumors have surfaced that the locals were actively involved in concealing her murder and burial site. Other reports show that the locals are intimidated by the suspect and would do anything in their power to not cross him. In 2008, a memorial plaque dedicated to Sinnott's memory was stolen from a cemetery in Wexford. The plaque, previously cemented to the wall, was stolen on the night before it was to be unveiled to the public.

The last person to be added to the list of missing women in the Vanishing Triangle case was Deirdre Jacob. This 18-year old native of Newbridge, County Kildare, was reported missing on July 28, 1998. She was staying in Twickenham, London, and taking her undergraduate studies at St. Mary's University. At the time of her disappearance, Deirdre was back in Ireland for summer break.

On the afternoon of her disappearance, Deirdre was running errands on Newbridge's high street when she visited a bank, the post office, and made a quick stop to her grandmother's newspaper and magazine shop across the road before walking home. She was just several yards from her parents' home (according to testimonies by passing motorists and pedestrians) but never made it to her front door.

Two months after her she went missing, the Gardaí found a link between her case and five other cases of missing women in the previous years. Operation Trace was launched to investigate the similarities between the cases. The other victims allegedly connected to the missing persons case of Deirdre include Annie McCarrick, JoJo Dollard, Fiona Pender, Ciara Breen, and Fiona Sinnott.

Deirdre's parents, Michael and Bernadette Jacobs, have repeatedly criticized the Gardaí for their lack of interest in their daughter's case and their sluggish progress in uncovering new information and following new leads. Although the case has gone cold over the past several years, rumors and new pieces of information regularly surface. They are aware of the various assumptions and theories surrounding their missing daughter's case. One of the most believed theories is Larry Murphy raping and murdering their daughter and several other missing women.

Larry Murphy, a convicted rapist and attempted murderer, was imprisoned for 15 years beginning in 2000. Subsequent to his arrest, Murphy became the suspect of many of the women's disappearance cases in the Vanishing Triangle. In 2000, he was charged with rape and attempted murder on an unnamed woman who was bound by Murphy and driven roughly 40 kilometers away into a remote area in a forest. He raped her four times and tried to strangle her to death before he was unintentionally thwarted by passing deer hunters. The hunters' car's headlights momentarily stunned the man, allowing his victim to flee and run towards their direction. They brought her to the closest police station where she testified that Murphy had committed the awful atrocities against her. He was arrested and tried in court before being sentenced to 15 years for rape and attempted murder. During his incarceration, there appeared to be a complete cease to young women disappearing in the Leinster area.

However, Michael and Bernadette remain unconvinced that Murphy was even involved in the case, despite the public's and police's strong belief that he put an end to their daughter's life. "We need people to refocus without the shadows of Larry Murphy," Michael told reporters.

From between 2000 and 2012, no substantial information was discovered or offered to the Gardaí, and most of the missing women's cases soon went cold. Larry Murphy was in jail and this supposedly put an end to all the disappearances and murders. However, in late October 2012, the people of Ireland found a renewed interest in the Vanishing Triangle case following the abduction and murder of a pregnant 30-year old native of Couny Laois. The woman, Aoife Phelan, disappeared as she was heading home from a friend's house. The remains of her body were found, and a 24-year old man named Robert Corbet was charged with murder. He as supposedly the father of her unborn child, and they had gotten into an argument in his home before murdering her. In 2014, he was sentenced to spend the remainder of his life behind bars.

To date, there are still posters and coverage on TV and radio regarding the Ireland's Vanishing Triangle cases. It's difficult for a country of that size to soon forget the terrible horrors that plagued its citizens for roughly six years. "People remember their names to this day," says Alan Bailey who helmed the Gardaí taskforce in charge of finding a link between the eight missing women, "because they went missing of a short time period in a certain part of the country and because they were normal people going about their everyday routine." Alan gave his opinion on the whole Vanishing Triangle ordeal to reporters, stating that, "The Deirdre Jacob case was particularly troubling because she disappeared in broad daylight during the afternoon and close to her home in Newbridge."

The unexplainable disappearances of several women in a short period of time could have been attributed to the lack of surveillance cameras. Alan spoke of the matter, saying, "In the case of Annie McCarrick, the only CCTV footage we have of her on the day she disappeared was in her local bank." If Annie were to disappear during this time and age of technology and public surveillance, then the authorities would have more information and be "far better placed to trace her movements."

The families of the victims show no signs of wanting to give up on their 20-year long search for their loved ones. If anybody has any information regarding the whereabouts of any of these women, please contact the Irish Police Force or members of their families.

MISSING BETHANY: THE TRUE STORY OF BETHANY DECKER

JENNY GREENWOOD

In many ways the life of Bethany Decker was not so different from others her age and who shared similar backgrounds. She worked full time as a waitress and attended college at George Mason University, majoring in Global Environmental Change. Sure, she was only 22 and married with one son, just 17-months-old. But that is hardly uncommon. And yes, her marriage was faltering, but even that was hardly unique, especially when married at such a young age to a husband serving repeated tours of duty in Afghanistan.

Nothing about Bethany seemed out of the ordinary.

Until she disappeared.

On January 29th, 2011 the young wife and mother vanished and has not been seen since.

What happened to Bethany Decker?

At the time of her disappearance, Bethany and her husband, Emile Decker had been married for 18 months. Their son was living with Bethany's mother, Kim Nelson, while Bethany focused on finishing her last semester at George Mason.

"She is my flip flops and lip gloss girl," her mother said, giving her that nickname because she was born in Hawaii. Bethany was a terrific student and graduated from high school with a 4.0 GPA. At the time of her disappearance she was only just a few credits shy of graduating from George Mason University. Her studies by day and her hard work as a waitress by night was about to pay off. With her degree she hoped to change the world in a positive way.

"Bethany was a physically attractive young woman," forensic psychologist Tim McGee said. "She was petite at four-foot-eleven and weighed 130 pounds. She was curvy and had a pretty face. Surely, she had more than her share of men who wanted to date her. Invariably, she attracted men who would be uncomfortable with dating someone who got a lot of attention from rivals."

As days and weeks passed with no contact, her family said they didn't begin to worry right away since the 21-year-old had such a hectic schedule. With Bethany away at college and working full-time it had not concerned her mother that she had not heard from her daughter in over three weeks. She tried calling on several occasions and was just directed to her voice-mail box.

"She had a seventeen-month old child at the time," McGee said. "But the child would stay with her in-laws. Still, those days where no one heard from her would suggest that they were used to not having her checking-in. So there is the possibility that there was some estrangement there."

Kim Nelson was not the only one struggling to get a hold of Bethany. One weekend Kim received a number of strange phone calls and some of Bethany's friends noticed unusual posts on Bethany's Facebook page.

"It was a Saturday morning and I had messages from four different people from different parts of the country that said, 'there's somebody on Facebook that's on Bethany's login, but it's not Bethany. It didn't sound like Bethany and didn't use terms Bethany would use. What's going on? Is there something wrong?'" Bethany's mother Kim said.

Kim immediately called her own parents to check on Bethany because they lived closer to her apartment in Ashburn, Virginia. Upon arrival, they noticed that Bethany's car was parked crooked, had a flat tire, and was dusty. This was peculiar because her grandparents drove past only one week prior and the car was parked differently.

The unused car, the Facebook posts, and the radio silence from Bethany formed mounting evidence that something was not quite right. But what finally inspired her family to call the police was when her grandparents knocked on her door and heard no answer.

"We just had a feeling. We were concerned," Evelyn Bayles, Bethany's grandmother said.

On February 19, 2011 Bayles called the local police dept. and investigators soon descended upon the apartment complex and interviewed every collateral contact in Bethany's life. But it had been at least three weeks since anyone had seen her. The only trace left behind was her dusty, double-parked car.

The vehicle was searched, but it left no clues as to where she might have disappeared to. Her apartment revealed nothing. It was entirely empty, except for a bag of her own clothes. There were no signs of foul play or a physical altercation. Her bank account had been static for weeks. Soon, the police organized search teams who prowled the nearby landscape with dogs and combed through dumpsters, looking for human remains. She had not shown up for her scheduled shift at Carrabba's Italian Grill in Centreville, VA, the popular restaurant chain where she worked, since the day she was last seen. She had disappeared without a trace.

"We want Bethany safe. We love her and we want to know that she is OK," Bethany's mother said to reporters. An investigator also noted that there was no evidence or indication that Bethany was not alive. But behind the investigator's affirmation, lay the disturbing truth that there was no activity on her bank account, email account, or cell phone records.

SUSPECT THE HUSBAND FIRST

At first, the disappearance seemed like an elaborate ruse engineered by Bethany's husband, Emile. According to police, Emile had seen Bethany the day before she disappeared. And despite finding no activity on her bank account, email account, or cell phone records, someone was still posting on her Facebook account.

Someone had her login information. Who better to suspect than her husband?

The investigators started to circle their wagons around Emile. The motive lined up all-too-well. He was a young man stuck serving in Afghanistan while quietly harboring suspicions that Bethany was being unfaithful. She had become pregnant again but was it even his child? One week before her disappearance, between Jan. 18 to Jan. 23, Bethany and Emile had vacationed in Hawaii in what was possibly a desperate last-ditch attempt to save their marriage. When that failed, the investigators speculated, Emile descended into a fit of rage and Bethany disappeared.

What buttressed this theory was that she was never at the airport to bid him farewell before he returned to Afghanistan on February 2nd 2011. His wife did not see him off, as she had multiple times before, investigators said. His fellow infantrymen thought this was peculiar but attributed it to the marital difficulties that Emile was experiencing.

Armed with this information, investigators were eager to interrogate Emile and did so within a few days of Bethany's disappearance.

"He is cooperating. He's answered several questions for us now," a spokesman for the police said. They did not have details of their conversation with Emile, but said they were trying to establish a more solid time line of when Bethany was last seen based on information from her husband.

But because Emile was serving in Afghanistan by the time the investigation started, investigators needed to contact U.S. military officials to arrange bringing him back home for further questioning and a polygraph test.

But Emile was not being named a suspect or a person of interest in the case.

"I don't want to limit him saying he's a suspect or a person of interest at this time. We're playing catch up on an investigation of a missing person, therefore, we would like to talk to as many people as possible," the police spokesman said.

"He wants to cooperate fully. He was very concerned of Bethany's whereabouts and condition. Obviously, being the father of their child he wants to hear a good resolution to this."

AN AFFAIR AT WORK

Bethany was having an affair with a man named Ronald Roldan, a Bolivian immigrant she met at Carrabba's Italian Grill. With that information, it wasn't inconceivable that the five-months pregnant Bethany was carrying Roldan's child. Investigators now had someone other than Emile with a possible motive in the case.

Roldan would also be the last person to see her in the Ashburn apartment on January 29th, 2011.

The two were reportedly living together in the Orchard Grass Terrace complex until the lease expired on Jan. 31, and from the very beginning, according to friends and family, the relationship was abusive. Bethany Decker met Roldan at a vulnerable time in her life according to her mother. She did not plan on being in a relationship with Roldan, nor staying in a relationship with him. When Nelson first met him, she found him to be charming. But friends and family soon learned that he turned controlling and even dangerous. Friends insisted that she check-in regularly with them as the relationship turned from emotionally abusive to physically abusive.

"The whole circumstance of her getting involved with Roldan is nuts," McGee said. "The media had to be careful not to judge her for behavior in having an affair because then that suggests that she brought on the violence to herself. But it is apparent that her mother knew about the affair."

Bethany had been desperately exploring a safe exit strategy from the relationship, according to her mother. But Roldan refused to leave and he would not let her leave either. She confided to her mother the danger that Roldan posed to her life, saying there was a time when Roldan threw her across the room and into a wall. He threatened to cut her open with car keys. Her family encouraged her to just walk away from the relationship, but she insisted that, "He'll never let it go. He'll find me."

Investigators believe that Bethany was in the Ashburn apartment the day she went missing because she made a commitment to work that evening at Carrabba's Italian Grill, not far away from Ashburn. But she never showed up for her scheduled shift, thus making Roldan the last person to see her that day.

In March 2011, only a few weeks after the initial investigation was launched, investigators searched Roldan's family home, where he was living with his mother and seized his immigration papers, a black bag with assorted documents, and other items, according to a search warrant filed in Fairfax County.

As the investigation progressed, investigators told reporters at the time that Roldan "made conflicting statements regarding when he noticed Bethany's car being parking in the parking lot in front of their shared apartment." Eventually, at some point during the investigation, detectives said Roldan stopped cooperating with law enforcement.

"Some are cooperative, some are not. We feel we have probably interviewed folks in this investigation already that probably have information that we would like to have and they've been reluctant to hand that information over. So, we're hopeful that, as the days go by, that they'll realize that if they have information, no matter how insignificant they think it is, they will give it to us," former Sheriff Steve Simpson told reporters in 2011. Bethany's mother, Nelson, believes that Sheriff Simpson was likely referring to Roldan's family members who were holding back on sharing pertinent information.

As investigators dug deeper into Roldan's past they found a violent criminal record that aligned perfectly with the alleged abuse in his relationship with Bethany. In one incident he smashed a woman's car windshield in a fit of rage. According to investigators, when they interviewed Roldan's other girlfriends prior to Bethany, he demonstrated a clear pattern of abuse.

On Friday, Aug. 5, 2011, the Loudoun County investigators released new photos of Bethany, hoping the images would generate new information as to her whereabouts. They clearly had not yet given up hope that she was still alive.

Bethany was due to give birth to her second child on Sunday, Aug. 7, and hope remained that somewhere, some hospital would recognize her if she were seeking medical treatment. "We're trying to get the picture out as to how she would look today," said a spokesman for the sheriff's office.

The photos released to the media showed Bethany when she was in the final trimester of pregnancy with her first child. A second photo showed an image of a tattoo just above her left ankle. For investigators, it was still the only path forward. "Nothing has led us in any other direction," an investigator said.

The investigation turned cold from there. It was clear that Bethany wasn't coming back. She was likely dead. Weeks turned into months and months into years. There were no new leads and no sign of

Bethany. It was not until 2014 that the case took an important twist-perhaps the most shocking clue of all which would lead many to conclude that Roldan had in fact murdered her.

In 2014 Roldan had moved on to a new relationship with another young woman, Vicky Willoughby. The same pattern of abuse that happened in his relationship with Bethany, as alleged by her friends and family, would also emerged in his new relationship. Willoughby ultimately moved to a new city, Pinehurst, NC to escape from her relationship with Roldan, but he soon followed her.

Police responded to a 911 call for a domestic violence incident at 1:30 a.m. on Nov. 12, 2014. Willoughby had shot Roldan in self-defense twice — once in the chest and once in the abdomen. But the weak stopping power of her .38 caliber handgun did not bring him down. Instead, Roldan charged forward and wrestled the gun out of Willoughby's hand and shot her three times, hitting her in the head and leg. Miraculously, she survived the shooting, but lost her right eye.

Four months later, Roldan was charged with the attempted murder of Willoughby. In addition to shooting her, Roldan also broke Willoughby's neck, bit her, and punched her.

Roldan took a plea deal in the case in May, 2015 and the charges were consolidated into one sentence, with a minimum of six years and a maximum of eight years and three months. Roldan pleaded guilty to two reduced charges — felony assault with a deadly weapon with intent to kill, inflicting serious injury, and felony assault inflicting serious bodily injury.

But with time served, he could be released as early as 2020. The Assistant District Attorney in the case, Peter Strickland, said he made the decision to accept the plea agreement during jury selection.

Presumably, after he finishes his prison sentence, U.S. Immigration and Customs Enforcement would take custody of Roldan to begin processing him for deportation back to Bolivia. But with millions of criminally convicted immigrants awaiting deportation approval from their host countries, his future status in the U.S. remains unclear.

As for Willoughby, she was astonished that an attempted murder case such as this would yield such a light sentence.

"I am disappointed in the gaps leading to technicalities and diminishing the consequences for such violence," Willoughby said. "This was not a first offense. Violent repeat offenders should be kept off the street. I fear for the next victim, in this country or another."

The other offense Willoughby was referring to, of course, was Bethany's disappearance. His arrest and subsequent plea-deal triggered red flags for those still investigating Bethany's disappearance. His pattern of controlling, obsessive behavior with women was apparent. But now there was actual, documented evidence of his capacity to cross the line from obsessive, stalking behavior into dangerous violence.

Bethany's mother had hoped for a longer sentence for Roldan. "There is no sentence that can equate to the terror and suffering caused by Ronald to Vicky and others, including Bethany," she told reporters, "I am hoping that him being behind bars will allow someone who has information about Bethany to come forward so there can be justice for Bethany. I pray that their heart would be moved to do the right thing so their [conscience will be] clear."

In cases such as these, prior convictions or arrests go a long way towards demonstrating an actual pattern of abuse. Most violent criminals have a long record of exhibiting violent behaviors and domestic abusers, in particular, have a history of controlling and obsessive behavior with their significant others, often punctuated by fits of rage and violence.

Domestic abuse is unlikely to end when the victim ends the relationship. In fact, it can often escalate when the abused victim tries to separate. The abusers will explode at the impending loss of control. Many murders of abused women occur during or after the separation, when the abuser feels the victim is escaping his control and he fails to re-establish it.

Research shows that the overwhelming number of domestic abusers are never arrested. Those that are arrested often had prior domestic violence arrests or orders of protection filed against them and fall into the category of serial domestic abusers. Additionally, only a very small percentage of those arrested for domestic violence had no prior criminal history at all.

Investigators never charged Roldan or named him as a suspect, but said he is no longer willing to answer questions about Bethany's disappearance and acknowledge that there are no other suspects. They also maintain that they have no evidence that suggests Decker is alive or dead.

One day after Roldan's guilty plea, on Friday, May 13, it was (or would have been) Bethany's 27th birthday. Nelson wished her daughter a happy birthday on her Facebook page and said, "We have been waiting a long time but will not lose hope."

Whether or not any further leads will develop in this case is unclear. But investigators, after five years, finally filed a search warrant requesting access to a cellphone, tablet and laptop belonging to Ronald Roldan. And buried within the search warrant, was a revealing quote from Roldan's ex-girlfriend, Willoughby, who told police Roldan once said, "I've made someone disappear before and I'll do it again."

So does the evidence implicate Roland in the disappearance and likely murder of Bethany Decker? Without actual forensic evidence or even definitive proof that she is dead, it is unlikely that any charges will be brought against Roldan. But what is almost certainly clear is that Roldan fit the pattern of a serial domestic abuser. The prior criminal convictions, the allegations of abuse from Bethany's family, and his refusal to submit to a polygraph test, makes him a a likely suspect in the court of public opinion.